The Lighthouses of Ireland

RICHARD M. TAYLOR

The Lighthouses
of Ireland

A PERSONAL HISTORY

FOREWORD BY JOHN DE COURCY IRELAND

The Collins Press

Published in 2004 by
The Collins Press
West Link Park
Doughcloyne
Wilton
Cork
This paperback edition published in 2006

This book is not intended as an aid to navigation.
The author and publisher disclaim any responsibility for errors
regarding light character.

British Library Cataloguing in Publication Data
Taylor, Richard M.
The lighthouses of Ireland: a personal history
1. Taylor, Richard M. 2. Lighthouses - Ireland 3.
Lighthouses
- Ireland - Maintenance and repair
I. Title
387.1'55'09415'092
ISBN-10 190517215X
ISBN-13 978-190517215X

Typesetting: Dominic Carroll

Font: Sabon 11 point

Cover design: Artmark

Printed in Malta

Cover photographs:
Front: Fanad Head lighthouse by Nigel Teggin
Back: Inishowen lighthouse by Nigel Teggin

Contents

continued over

Photo Credits

Preface

I once heard a man say his ambition was to visit every lighthouse in Ireland – a formidable task indeed. I wonder was he aware of just how many lighthouses there are around our coastline. The majority of us, with even the slightest interest in nautical matters, will have heard of such places as the Fastnet, Baily, Loop Head or the Hook, but where are the Maidens, Rotten Island, Straw Island, the Bull or Cromwell Point?

Many of our lighthouses, especially those erected on rocks, are not accessible to the general public. There are, however, many mainland stations that can be easily reached, yet often the traveller or tourist will pass nearby without realising how close they are to a lighthouse and a little bit of history.

As a technician working for the Commissioners of Irish Lights, I was fortunate to visit and work in practically every lighthouse on our coast. Some of the people I came to know and some of the history of the lights they tended are presented here in this personal account of the lighthouses of Ireland. To you the reader, and to the gentleman mentioned above, I wish bon voyage.

Richard M. Taylor
October 2004

Foreword

I have been reading books about the sea for more than 70 years, and reviewing maritime books for national newspapers and international maritime journals for upwards of 40 years. I can say, without hesitation, that this book ranks well within the top dozen of all these books by the satisfaction that reading it provided.

The great value of this book is that it is written by one who really knows what he is writing about, for he spent a lifetime in the lighthouse service and had personal experience, weeks at a time, of the most remote and, to most people, unheard of lighthouses and harbour lights. The notable feature of Mr Taylor's book is that there is not a dull moment in it. He has succeeded in making the technicalities of lighthouse engineering clear and comprehensible, he has a quite wonderful sense of scenery and of the unparalleled beauty and fathomless malignity of the sea, and he can give as clear and vivid a picture of a lighthouse keeper's mentality as the silhouette of a ship caught in the million-candle-power light beam of the Fastnet or the Tuskar.

Moreover, he has thrown gleaming light on an age of coast-lighting technique that reached its apogee when he was working, and now is drastically changed with automation.

But do not think that the book is all about lighthouse keepers and their lighthouses, embellished though it is by many a hair-raising and many a sly and amusing tale. It is also the unique record by a hugely observant, intelligent and reflective mind of the imperceptible, at first, but eventually omnipotent changes which have affected every far distant and not-so-far-distant coastal areas of our island, from Antrim to Wexford and from Donegal to Kerry.

John de Courcy Ireland

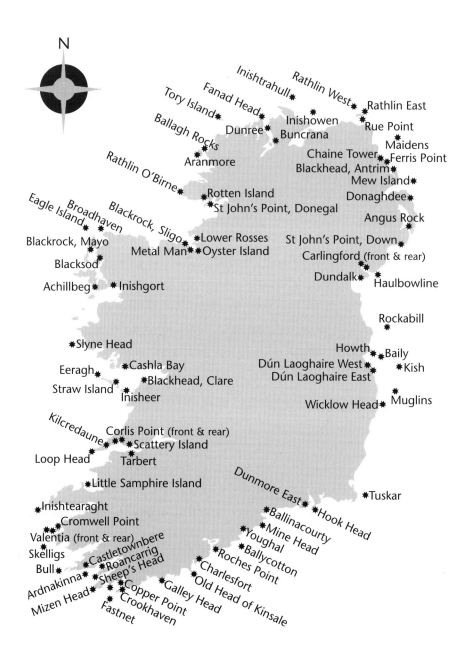

N

Inishtrahull
Rathlin West
Fanad Head
Tory Island
Rathlin East
Ballagh Rocks
Inishowen
Rue Point
Dunree
Buncrana
Maidens
Chaine Tower
Ferris Point
Blackhead, Antrim
Rathlin O'Birne
Aranmore
Mew Island
Rotten Island
Donaghdee
St John's Point, Donegal
Eagle Island
Broadhaven
Blackrock, Sligo
Angus Rock
Blackrock, Mayo
Lower Rosses
St John's Point, Down
Metal Man
Oyster Island
Carlingford (front & rear)
Blacksod
Dundalk
Achillbeg
Inishgort
Haulbowline

Rockabill

Slyne Head
Howth
Baily
Eeragh
Cashla Bay
Dún Laoghaire West
Kish
Straw Island
Blackhead, Clare
Dún Laoghaire East
Inisheer
Wicklow Head
Muglins

Kilcredaune
Corlis Point (front & rear)
Scattery Island
Loop Head
Tarbert
Little Samphire Island
Dunmore East
Tuskar
Inishtearaght
Ballinacourty
Hook Head
Cromwell Point
Mine Head
Valentia (front & rear)
Youghal
Skelligs
Castletownbere
Ballycotton
Bull
Roancarrig
Roches Point
Ardnakinna
Sheep's Head
Charlesfort
Mizen Head
Copper Point
Galley Head
Old Head of Kinsale
Crookhaven
Fastnet

Guide to Light Character

Each lighthouse has its own specific light character; that is, the colour, sequence, timing and other characteristics specific to each light, such as whether it is fixed or flashing, isophase or occulting, and so on. Each entry in this book is accompanied by details of the light's character (abbreviations are explained below).

It is important to state that Irish Lights and other authorities periodically alter light characteristics as and when considered necessary, and that a lighthouse may be discontinued after the publication of this book, or new lights may be commissioned. The author and publisher therefore disclaim any responsibility for errors regarding light character included, and strongly advise readers that this book should not be used as an aid to navigation.

The total period (complete sequence of light plus eclipse) is stated in seconds

Fl   Flashing (the period of light is shorter than the period of eclipse)

Fl (2) Group flashing (the number in brackets indicates the number of flashes)

Lfl   Long flash (a single flash of not less than 2s regularly repeated)

Qfl   Quick flash (a light which flashes at a rate of 50–80 flashes per minute)

Iso   Isophase (the period of light is equal to the period of eclipse)

Oc   Occulting (the period of light is longer than the period of eclipse)

Dir   Directional light (a light showing over a very narrow sector; this sector may be flanked by sectors of different colour or character, or greatly reduced intensity)

W   White

R   Red

G   Green

*   Shown throughout 24 hours

**   High intensity light by day

Also shown by day when fog signal is sounding

Also shown by day in poor visibility

South Coast

Hook Head

The first I ever heard of a lighthouse was when a very patient teacher attempted to instil in me a sense of the grandeur of edifices of bygone days, particularly the Seven Wonders of the Ancient World; that lighthouse is the Pharos in Alexandria. The oldest functioning lighthouse is the Tower of Hercules at La Coruna, said to have been built in pre-Roman times, but in all probability reconstructed many times since. This brings us neatly to our claim to possessing the oldest working lighthouse in these islands. Built in the twelfth century, the Hook Tower in Wexford is thought to have been the work of William Fitzgerald of Carew Castle in Pembrokeshire, better known as Strongbow's brother-in-law. Built as a defended lighthouse, its walls are up to 2.6 metres thick. The steps to the top of the tower – 31 metres from the ground – are built into the walls. The structure is an impressive 12.2 metres in diameter.

The Church in medieval times was closely involved with many primitive lights, including that at Hook Head. The original light on the peninsula was where the ruin of St Saviour's church at Churchtown-over-Hook now stands. St Dubhain of Wales built his oratory there in the fifth century, and such was his concern for the seafarers around this treacherous coast, he built a sort of mini-tower from which an iron basket filled with coal, wood or tar kept his light going under all weather conditions.

The original name in Irish of Hook Head is Rinn-Dubhain, meaning 'Point of Dubhain'. When the English settlers came centuries later, the name St Dubhain was forgotten and Hook Head came into use. After the saint died, the light was maintained by his religious community, but later, when the Order of St Augustine was founded, the monk from the primitive Celtic monastery of St Dubhain became canon of the order. As St Augustine's Order had the care and maintenance of the present tower, the light of St Dubhain was discontinued and the present light came into being. It fell into disuse early in the seventeenth century, and no light was exhibited there again until 1665. Various bodies, among them the Kilmainham Hospital Authorities, the Commissioners of Public Revenue and – later – the Ballast Office, took control of the light, and the present lantern was erected in 1864. This superseded a similar one of 1791.

There were many ships wrecked off the Hook; perhaps the most notable was a collier owned by Heiton's of Dublin, which collided with another vessel just off Hook Head on 7 December 1919. All fourteen crew members were lost. Seven bodies were found on Bannow Strand; oddly enough, all were wearing life jackets.

As is the case with many of our older lighthouses, the Hook has its share of ghostly happenings, and many a scary yarn is told of keepers going up to wind the light and seeing some long-departed occupant of the tower sitting in the lantern, smoking his pipe. We had our quarters

Hook Head

in one of the tower rooms for many years (known to all of us, for some strange reason, as Liberty Hall), and while not given unduly to heroics, I can honestly say I never saw or felt any mysterious presence.

Whatever about ghosts, there was a principal keeper who did manage to keep me awake many a night. Bill Hamilton was a great one for yarns. He was a tall, bespectacled man, with an ash-laden cigarette forever dangling from his lips. Bill would have to pass my room on the way to wind his light – a mechanism that operated not unlike a grandfather clock, and which had to be seen to every 40 minutes. Bill's yarns were so long that by the time he had finished one, it was time to wind up again. Warning me not to go to bed, he would bound up the stairs, do his wind, and come back down again. As he lived in a separate house from the tower, it often transpired that he would spend all his watch with me. He was one of the great characters, a wizard at wireless and a genius of inventiveness. He even made a set of teeth for himself out of the bone handle of a knife. He generally put them in for Mass on Sundays.

In those days, the keeper's family was driven to church in the contractor's car. Bill was fond of his jar, and would tell me on the quiet to ask him in for one after Mass. On our way home after the service, just as we were about to pass the little pub at Templetown, I would say the required words and, amid dire looks from the others, the two of us would go into the packed kitchen of the pub. We would not be there long when the horn of the car would be sounded and, after ignoring it a few times, Bill would reluctantly go to the door and proclaim to all and sundry that it was a sad day when a friend could not ask him in for a drink without the whole bloody country knowing about it. Of course, I would get dark looks from his wife and the other abstainers for the rest of the week for leading the poor man astray. These little forays seem not to have done him any harm, as he died – a few years ago – at an advanced age, I am glad to say.

The Hook today is a squat, white, black-banded tower, topped off by a rather out-of-character modern lantern. Considering it first exhibited its naked flame back in the twelfth century, one cannot but be impressed at how this durable lighthouse has stood the test of time. Today, the light – with a range of 23 nautical miles – is automated; its character is a white flash every 3 seconds. An interpretive centre is being planned within the compound, and guided tours will enable visitors to relive the lightkeeper's life and isolation.

Before we leave this area, we must pay a brief visit to two discontinued lights that were once important to Duncannon. Aside from lights exhibited from ecclesiastical towers, many military installations, especially those guarding the entrances to harbours, were used not alone as navigational aids but also for sending important messages inland. Both Duncannon Fort and Charles Fort in Kinsale exhibited lights from their turrets. Both lights at Duncannon were of modern origin, and up to recent years were operated by means of carbide gas, which worked on much the same principle as the old carbide bicycle lamp. Water was allowed drop into the carbide at suitable intervals, thereby making sufficient gas to operate a light. At one time, many of these lighthouse generators were in use, especially in the smaller lighthouses. The generators were fitted with a bellows, which in turn operated a charging valve, only allowing sufficient carbide into the water chamber for immediate use. The light was much more brilliant than either electric or any of its counterparts. But difficulty in maintenance and obtaining replacement parts hastened their demise, and there are none of these excellent lights in operation today. The last generator is still kept at Charles Fort in Kinsale, but only as a museum piece.

The two lights at Duncannon were operated for many years by Bob White, and I – being of the vintage carbide era – knew Bob very well. He and his wife, Annie, became great friends of mine and I spent many happy days in Duncannon with them. Bob taught me how to ground fish and, with it, the art of patience. I can see him now, squatting on his favourite rock by the corner of the beach under the fort light, sucking on a battered stump of a pipe. Hour after hour he would sit there, waiting on that elusive nibble which would indicate a strike. Then came just the right amount of pressure on the rod and Bob would draw in his fish. He never lost any and, indeed, before the catch came into sight, he would know exactly what specimen it was. That is something I have yet to learn.

The fort at Duncannon is still used as a training ground for our army personnel, and one immaculately turned-out soldier comes to mind. His name was Furlong, and I used to make up a foursome for the game of solo in his billet. There, one could see rows of the most highly polished boots and shoes imaginable. I observed him one day at his polishing routine. Having applied the polish, he would rub vigorously and at amazing speed with the palm of his hand, and assured me that no dampness could possibly penetrate. A dual purpose was thus served in both obtaining and preserving a highly polished finish. He initiated me into this art, and I became quite expert at it.

On the way out of Duncannon village, pause at the top of the hill where you will see a gate on the seaward side of the road leading down to the north lighthouse. Take a stroll down this short boreen and marvel at the ingenuity it took to carve a lighthouse out of the side of the hill. In front of the tower there is a rampart giving an uninterrupted view over Waterford Harbour, bounded on the east by the Hook and on the west by Dunmore East. Although an unmanned lighthouse for many years, many former keepers will still remember happy days there as children. Indeed, it had been thought quite possible that one of these very children would return some day and take over as attendant, and the cycle would continue. But it's not to be. ✳W 3 seconds

Dunmore East

On the other side of Waterford Harbour, we come upon Dunmore East, another of the harbour lights controlled by Irish Lights. The pier-end lighthouse at Dunmore East was designed and built in 1826 by a Scotsman named Alexander Nimo; as far as is known, this was the only one built by him, though in his capacity as engineer for the western region of Ireland he was also responsible for the construction of many fine harbours on that stretch of coastline. Dunmore East has an excellent cast-iron railing around its lantern that has withstood the passage of time surprisingly well. The outlets for the flue pipes – in use when the lights had oil lamps – still survive.

On our way west, let us pause at a structure that is not a lighthouse but which is very familiar to the thousands that invade Tramore every summer – this is the famous 'metal man'. The original Admiralty signal tower was erected on Brownstown Head, but as this could easily be mistaken for the Hook Tower, it was suspected as the cause of many shipwrecks in the area – in bad weather, ships would enter Tramore Bay instead of Waterford Harbour. After many years of indecision, it was decided to have five towers in the area: two on Brownstown Head and three on Great Newtown Head, so as to distinguish one head from another and to avoid confusion with the single tower at Hook. The middle tower, on Newtown, supports the giant metal figure of a sailor with outstretched arm pointing away from the land out to sea. This tower, or beacon, is 18 metres in height and 6 metres in diameter. Since 1824, its intrepid master has worked tirelessly for his fellow mariners, and in bad weather is even said to chant, 'Keep off good ship, keep off from me for I am the rock of misery.' There is also a legend that if any maiden can hop around the beacon three times on one foot, she is sure to be married within the year. Pity so few of this admirable breed survive today! ✴ *Fl WR 8s*

Ballinacourty

Before going on to Mine Head, about 9 miles from Dungarvan, let us visit Ballinacourty lighthouse, only a few miles on the other side of the town. Hardly known, except to the locals and our own personnel, it is a lovely, quiet little station boasting no pretensions, but nonetheless well worth a visit for the peace and serenity of its surroundings.

✷ ✷ *Fl (2) WRG 10s*

Mine Head

Hardly any of the many students studying Irish in the nearby college of Ring know of the existence of the lighthouse at Mine Head. If, however, one gets as far as the quaintly named village of Old Parish, one is very close to it indeed. The highest lighthouse above sea level in Ireland, its tower, at 81 metres in elevation, was built in 1851. Its 2.5 million candelas has a range of 28 nautical miles. As a guideline, all lighthouses have their light power measured by reference to multiples of the light given out by the humble candle.

My memories of Mine Head are very pleasant ones. I hardly ever stayed in the lighthouse quarters, as they always seemed to be occupied. This was one of the land stations which had only two keepers, but had extra keepers for the long winter nights. I always stayed in a little shop at the crossroads, belonging to Mrs Power, whose husband was one of the local blacksmiths. The first time I stayed was shortly after the Rural Electrification Scheme had come to the area. The man who carried out the work stayed in the house; hence, it boasted every electrical appliance possible. But on enquiring as to the whereabouts of the toilet, Mrs Power proudly said they were very well equipped in that department and had one in every field – and that was how it remained for the very many times I stayed there, though that was quite a time ago.

Every night, we played cards. Middle-aged bachelors with names like 'The Doctor', 'The Priest' and 'The Pope' would come into the little shop to play the game of 45. Although quite a good card player, I soon found myself outclassed, as sign language was very much the order of the day. A wink, a touch of the ear or a cough could indicate any particular card, and I found it hard to get a partner. But it was not too long before I became as adept as any of them, and when ratings soared, there was no shortage of partners.

The area around Old Parish seemed to be completely devoid of eligible ladies, while nearby Dungarvan boasted the loveliest of women. Mrs Power had a daughter, but she was very young, and the bachelors and I were having rather a lean time of it. One night during a card game, however, the half-door opened to admit a vision. Cards and tricks were forgotten as we all stared in disbelief at this very delectable creature. Suddenly realising this vision was very real indeed, I quickly made room for her on the seat beside me, and under the baleful stares of the other bachelors managed to 'make contact'. After cards, I made a speedy exit, but it being a very dark night I could barely make out the form ahead of me. I put an arm around the figure who, to my dismay, turned out to be an old aunt of hers. Explaining how she was in charge of the girl for the few days she was home on holidays from England, and mumbling something about 'ships that pass in the night', I left her and went back to the digs, disgusted. Very soon, my indiscretion was common knowledge, and I was the butt of some humorous but caustic jokes for quite a while afterwards. I have not been to Mine Head for some years now. I wonder do they still play cards in that little house, and whatever happened to all those lovely people? Happy days, indeed.

✷ ✷ *Fl (4) W 20s*

So we travel to Youghal, whose lighthouse has the distinction of being practically on a main street. My earliest recollection of Youghal is when I was very young and quite unimpressed by anything resembling a lighthouse. I was born in Mallow, County Cork – very far from the sea. My mother and father would take us there for our 'annual holidays'. My father, who was a permanent-way inspector on the railway, would get 'privilege tickets'. Obtained at greatly reduced prices, this concession was much appreciated given that there were eight of us children. So once a year, on a memorable Sunday, buckets and spades, paraphernalia of all descriptions and crates of sandwiches were hiked up to Mallow station as we embarked on our great adventure. Changing stations at Cork was an event in itself. Once in Youghal, we splashed and cavorted in the sea until utterly exhausted. My parents would paddle for hours, and my father would be convinced that his feet would be trouble-free for the rest of the year. He would exhort us children to take enormous gulps of sea air to counteract the effect of the town's pollution – this at a time when Mallow boasted of a mere four cars, property of the priest, the doctor, the sergeant and the vet. Looking out the carriage window as we departed Youghal, we would wave enthusiastically to the kids sitting on the railway bridge, and I was certain they must all be children of millionaires that they could afford to stay the night in Youghal. Happy, innocent days, and despite many more elaborate holidays since, the excitement of those magical Sundays will never be surpassed.

But back to our lighthouse. Hidden behind an elevated wall on the way out to the Strand Road, only its dome is visible to the casual observer. It does not present a remarkable appearance, but this lighthouse has an historic background. The first tower, built in 1190 by Fitzgerald, a

Norman conqueror, was in ecclesiastical hands until around 1542. There is evidence that the nuns of St Ann's convent looked after it for many years. There is a place called St Ann's Head at the entrance to the bay of Milford Haven in Wales, and it can be assumed this order also had charge of the light there. In those days, of course, the only lights available were naked flames, and one must marvel at the efforts this remarkable order of nuns made and the hardships they endured to ensure the safety of mariners.

The old tower at Youghal was called 'The Nunnery', but following the abolition of the monasteries around the middle of the sixteenth century, the light fell into disuse. The present lighthouse is built on precisely the same site. The locals will be proud to show you the field near the lighthouse where – it is alleged – Sir Walter Raleigh, the town's lord mayor in 1588, planted the first potatoes in Europe.

I have very happy memories of the various times I stayed in the dwelling house attached to the lighthouse. My only unpleasant experience was when, as the only single man available, I was obliged to travel there from Dublin on Christmas Eve to correct a fault in the lighting apparatus, which had been left temporarily in the care of the one of the locals. I did not see much of Christmas that year. ✳ *Fl WR 2.5s*

Ballycotton

If you have ever been to the pretty seaside village of Ballycotton, there is no need to point you in the direction of the lighthouse, as it's impossible to miss the striking rock just off the harbour on which the lighthouse is built, with its black tower and lantern enclosed by white walls. I think this must be many a layman's idea of a lighthouse, though the colour is somewhat unusual.

The lighthouse nearly wasn't built at Ballycotton. During the mid-nineteenth century, local merchants and shipowners had lobbied for a light on Capel Island, south of Youghal, but following the loss of the *Sirius* in 1847, it was decided to construct a lighthouse at Ballycotton. The tower was built in 1851, is 60 metres in elevation, and the light – at nearly 250,000 candelas – is visible for 20 nautical miles.

There was one very elaborate dwelling house built on Ballycotton Rock a few years ago, but the locals must have thought a luxury hotel was being built, it took so long to complete. Given that most of the materials had to be landed by helicopter, the project posed quite a few problems and proved a very expensive exercise. ✴*Fl WR 10s#*

Roches Point

Guarding the entrance to Cork Harbour is Roches Point lighthouse. Built in 1817, it is a mere 30 metres above sea level. The original lighthouse here was dismantled and re-erected at Duncannon North in 1838. Close by is the village of Whitegate – as sleepy a place it always was despite the location there of the oil refinery.

If we were to sail into the harbour, we would arrive at one of the few pile structures off our coast. This is the Spit Bank in Cobh. These piles were built from iron and timber, and were scientifically constructed bearing in mind their vulnerability to the elements. At one time the Spit Bank was considered one of our most important lights, guiding as it did the great liners that came into Cobh and which brought such prosperity to the town. Alas, those days are no more and, like many of its counterparts, Cobh now rests on its past glory.

I was a frequent visitor to the Spit Bank in those days of the liners. The attendant was a man called Mike Cotter. I thought he was old the first time I saw him, but in subsequent years he always looked the same. Short, powerful and silent, he could communicate more than most with just a squirt of tobacco juice. He and his wife lived in a little house in the Holy Ground. They had no children. Mike was most disdainful of any mechanical aid for getting to his lighthouse, and once told me that he had rowed the equivalent of the journey to America and back – twice! I once offered to use the spare oar to help him row the boat, but the baleful glance I received ensured I would never again offend him with such an ignominious suggestion. Although his wife had never been at the lighthouse, she could discuss every aspect of the plant and lighting apparatus, and it was uncanny to listen to her discussing the faults which could occur from time to time. This was the only job Mike had, and the salary being very small meant he was often in dire straits. So when a well-off brother in the States decided to come home to die, Mike was elated. Despite his meagre funds, Mike fed the fellow so well that, alas, he soon got better and went back to America. Mike and his wife did not survive too long afterwards. We gave away his lighthouse some years ago to the Cork Harbour Board. I wonder what Mike would have said about that.

It would be unworthy of me to leave this area without some mention of the Daunt light-ship, as I had the dubious distinction of almost sinking her. Never having been on a ship before, by some strange quirk of fate I found myself en route to the Daunt – off the coast of County Cork – to rectify a fault in the engine room. These jobs were usually carried out by what was called the 'Heavy Squad', but all being otherwise engaged, I was elected for the trip, the 'powers that be' conveniently overlooking the fact that I had never been on a ship before. So off to Cobh with me, and on that first visit I remember staying in the Seamen's Hostel for three shillings – my own private room with breakfast provided. It was difficult to find digs in Cork in those days, as the passenger service in and out of the port was usually very heavy. But we were always sure of a bed in the hostel, and there was no extra charge for the prayers provided by our hosts!

The next morning, I purchased enough provisions for the ten-day trip. After waiting on the pier for hours for two of the crew who had been on a binge all night and who were dumped out of a taxi, we set off for the Daunt. We had hardly left the pier when I got sick, and that's the way I stayed for the entire trip.

Moored light-ships have a very special method of making you sick in a way no moving vessel has. On bad days, and all of them were bad, it strains and heaves at its moorings, rolls and dips, and unleashes such mighty shudders that one feels for certain the ship is coming apart. I know experienced deep-sea sailors who die a death for the first few days on board. However, a job had to be done, and after being ill for five days in the bunk, the skipper gave me a couple of his men, and I crawled down to the engine room. In my befuddled state, the only way I could see to do the repair job was to take off the sea-cock. The two crewmen exchanged glances – it was obvious they did not think much of that idea. They patiently explained to me that we were below sea level in the engine room, and if the sea-cock was taken off, water would pour in and we would all be drowned. I could not quite comprehend this, and anyway why should they tell *me* my job? As I proceeded to dismantle the sea-cock, one fellow grabbed me while the other bounded up the stairs. Next thing I knew, the skipper and all the crew were in the engine room, and I can tell you the language was indeed choice. I was lucky I wasn't thrown overboard. I don't know who completed the task I had been sent to undertake, but I returned to the bunk until the relief boat was due.

All I had for the ten days on that ship was a bottle of Bovril. When the relief boat eventually arrived, one of the sailors gave me a letter for his girlfriend in the Rob Roy pub in Cobh, and assured me I would be given a large brandy as an instant cure for my condition. Being very abstemious in those days and quite unaware of the potency of brandy, I drank the lot neat and promptly collapsed on the floor. The poor girl thought I was dead, but I was on the first train out of Cobh the following morning, making sure to put as much distance as possible between myself and the Daunt. In the course of my career, I have had to travel on many ships. I do not get sick any more and try not to sink any of them, but that first trip to the Daunt left me with a permanent dislike of ships and – I might add – of Bovril. ✳ *Fl WR 3s#*

Charlesfort

Charlesfort is located just outside the town of Kinsale, from where King James II disembarked prior to his Boyne campaign. One of my favourite places until it became commercialised, I knew Kinsale when the harbour boasted only one small boat, which belonged to a local merchant. The town was derelict and forgotten, and one could easily acquire a house. A conglomerate moved in soon after, and built the Trident Hotel on stilts over the water. The boat marina followed and the result is that, today, Kinsale has become the ultimate in sophistication. Yet despite its smart hotels, gourmet restaurants and exclusive clientele, I doubt if this charming little place will ever lose its unique character. Not many seaside towns were built with such utter abandon, and its quaint narrow streets are reminiscent of a bygone age. It is hard to conceive that at one time, the sea covered practically the entire centre of the town, but there are the remains of a lighthouse as proof of this. Called the 'Cuckold lighthouse', its remnants can be seen at the end of the Long Quay just under the Cork Gate. Built in the twelfth century, it had other uses: it is known that at various times it served as a mill and as a prison.

We will leave the town and go by way of Scilly to the charming hamlet of Summercove. With barely enough room for two cars to pass, it eventually opens up and we come upon the magnificent Charlesfort, built in the late seventeenth century on the site of the former Ringcurran Castle, and set alight in 1922 following the departure of the British army. Deep within its recesses is the diminutive lighthouse which is the pride and joy of Irish Lights. Superbly maintained by Michael Arnott for many years, it was one of the last lighthouses on the coast to use carbide for its light. Incidentally, Michael's father, Bob, was the skipper on the Daunt light-ship during my abortive 'innocent aboard' trip. Two previous lights had been built within Ringcurran Castle (known locally as Barry Óg's Castle). The first was the cottage-type, mentioned previously; later, when the fort was built, a light was exhibited from a diamond-shaped aperture on top of one of the high walls. Incidentally, this window is still there and well preserved. The fort itself is well worth a visit, and the people who have been restoring it for years are to be complimented on a fine job. The history of the fort is excellently presented in an exhibition chamber, and there are frequent tours. ✳Fl WRG 5s*

Old Head of Kinsale

Leaving the town of Kinsale, we travel to the Old Head of Kinsale. It often surprised me that many visitors to the area seemed to be totally unaware of its existence, yet the superb scenic beauty of the peninsula would be hard to surpass.

There are actually three lighthouses built on the head. To fully appreciate the serenity of the surroundings, one needs to walk across the head rather than drive. About halfway, the remains of a small, cottage-type lighthouse can be seen, the best preserved of its type. It is well worth inspection, and though the stairs have disintegrated somewhat, access can be gained to the roof from the outside. There appears to have been ample accommodation for the lightkeeper and his family. As mentioned before, the light was exhibited from a fire platform built on a pillar projecting through the roof, and remains of the fuel used for the light were recently found at the site. Built in 1665, it was noted in 1703 that the light had not been lit for twenty years. In 1804, Thomas Forge, the lighthouse builder, replaced the coal-burning light-set with a small-diameter temporary lantern with twelve oil lamps and reflectors. By 1810, the reflectors were non-existent.

When it was decided to build another lighthouse the more usual round tower was deemed the most suitable for this exposed headland. Similar to the Baily, it was built a little way to the east of the cottage light, and first showed its light on 16 May 1814. In 1849, however, a survey of the head was carried out, and it was decided to reposition the lighthouse at the end of the peninsula. This was duly done, and the present lighthouse – a striking black-and-white tower – came into operation on 1 October 1853. It has an elevation of 72 metres and its 750,000-candelas light has a range of 25 nautical miles.

The Old Head light is of vital importance, controlling as it does the entrance to Cork Harbour. It is often cited in reference to the sinking of the *Lusitania* in 1915, a tragedy that occurred not too far off the head. There are frequent visits to the lighthouse by the relatives of those who drowned, making their private pilgrimages to the nearest point of land.

Life at the Old Head has changed enormously over the years. When the lightkeepers lived permanently with their families at the station they were totally integrated into the local community. Yet theirs was a fascinating lifestyle. Together with the families of the nearby coastguard station, they formed a colony all to themselves. I recently read a poignant account by a man whose father was posted to the staff of Lloyd's signal station, under which name the coastguard station was then known. The year was 1917, and he recalled the happy school days spent with the children from the lighthouse. Life seemed to have been idyllic, as they searched for seagulls' eggs, fished for mackerel, pollock and bream in the Cush and Gunhole coves, and fetched fresh water from the spring over the cliffs at Gunhole. Water was also obtained from the rainfall on the roofs and taken down through the guttering to large storage tanks, as is the case in most lighthouses. This water had to be boiled before consumption, so the spring water was used sparingly. They milked their own goats, made butter and cheese, and would seem to have been self-sufficient in many ways. The isolation and almost complete lack of transport would have made this necessary.

When the Troubles came in 1920, however, life altered dramatically for the English families at the coastguard station. The children were no longer welcome at the local school of Garrylucas, and one particular child had to go to school in Kinsale. Being of immature years, he found this incomprehensible. Shortly after, in 1922, the coastguard station closed down, and with it a way of life of which I personally would love to have been a part. ✶*Fl (2) W 10s*#

Galley Head

Galley Head lies approximately 5 miles southeast of Rosscarbery, County Cork, and is the southernmost point of a headland known as Dundeady Island, though joined to the mainland by an isthmus, on top of which is the ruined Dundeady (Dún na dTéide) Castle.

Two attempts were made – in 1849 and 1857 – to establish a lighthouse on Galley Head, each time with the Board's approval, but both were turned down by Trinity House. It did agree to sanction a local light, which would not be a burden on trading vessels. Fourteen years elapsed before Galley Head was mentioned again, this time by Lord Bandon in a letter to the Board, calling its attention to the number of wrecks off the headland. A number of other letters on the same subject was received around the same time. The Board checked the number of wrecks with Admiral Forbes, commander-in-chief of the British navy at Queenstown (now Cobh), and the subject was referred to the Inspecting Committee, which reported in March 1871. A copy of the report, together with correspondence, was forwarded to the Board of Trade in London, which in turn forwarded the information to Trinity House. Sanction from both bodies in London was received in April, and it is recorded that towards the end of May, Lord Bandon and the inhabitants of Rosscarbery expressed thanks to the 'elder brethren' and the Board

Galley Head

for sanctioning a lighthouse on Galley Head. The acquisition of land for the lighthouse, together with an access right of way, was negotiated over a period of two years, and was sealed in 1873. The contract for the buildings, including the tower but not the lantern, went to William M. Murphy of Bantry, and was carried out between 1873 and 1875.

Both the gas house and its brick chimney have survived the test of time and the elements surprisingly well. Around this time, there was great interest in the use of gas from channel coal as a source of illumination for optics, and Galley Head is another of those lighthouses whose original source of light was man-made gas. Messrs J. Edmundson and Company of Dublin, with its engineer, John R. Wigham, were forerunners in promoting this form of lighting, and supplied the gas-making plant, lantern and French-manufactured optic. The station was designed by Mr John S. Sloane, chief engineer, and consisted of a tower connected by a 38-metre-long corridor to the semi-detached, two-storey dwelling for the gas maker and to the gasworks located behind the dwelling.

The light was established on 1 January 1878, with a character of six or seven flashes in 16 seconds, followed by a 44-second period of darkness. This somewhat unusual character was due to the combination of an eight-sided optic revolving once every minute and the multiple jet gas burners being turned on and off approximately once every 2 seconds. Consequently, it was possible for vessels in certain positions to miss one of the flashes.

The tower, 21 metres high, was and still is painted white, as are the lantern and dome. The focal plane of the light is 53 metres above high water, and the original light could be seen in clear weather for 19 nautical miles. Six-and-a-half faces of the lantern have clear glazing covering a seaward bearing 256 degrees through west to 065 degrees. Nine-and-a-half faces are blanked off towards the land, except for six panes in two faces which have been left clear. The reason for these clear panes creating a landward arc goes back to the time when the Sultan of Turkey was staying with Lord Carbery at Castlefreke, or so the story goes. The visiting dignitary suggested that the light could be made to shine over the land so as to bring a kind of solace to the lives of the inhabitants. Lord Carbery must have had friends in the right places because the end result was that four panes on two sides were fitted with clear glass. The story does not end there, for after the light was converted to electricity in 1969, Mr A.D.H. Martin, the chief engineer, directed that the panes should be painted out so the much brighter light would not create a dazzling hazard to local motorists. Two months later, Dr M.D. Hegarty of Rosscarbery, backed by a number of local people, asked if they could have the light flashing towards land again, though at diminished strength. This was agreed, and two of the top-tier landward panes were made clear.

After the Inspecting Committee's tour in 1904, it was recommended that the light and optic be converted from quadriform gas to biform incandescent paraffin, giving a group of five flashes every 20 seconds. Trinity House and the Board of Trade gave their sanction the following year, and when the light was exhibited on 18 June 1907, its candela was increased to 362,000 and its range to 24 nautical miles.

The 1963 Inspecting Committee recommended converting the light to electricity and making the station unwatched, manned by a principal keeper. Conversion to electricity was on 20 August 1969, when the candle power increased from 362,000 to 2,800,000, with a range of 28 nautical miles.

Automation is inevitable for all, and the Galley Head in 1974 was no exception. It meant driving the optic with a gearless pedestal and setting up a monitoring system in the attendant's dwelling. This was carried out in 1979, following the principal keeper's retirement, who 'put on a new hat' to become the attendant. ✳ *Fl (5) W 20s*

Copper Point

As with so many of our lighthouses, the story at Copper Point begins with the intervention of a bigwig – in this case, and not for the first time, Lord Bandon. Some of his many acres were located around this part of west Cork, and in 1860 he wrote to the Board of Trade to request the construction of 'a conspicuous beacon' on Long Island in Roaringwater Bay. An Inspecting Committee was duly dispatched and found itself in agreement with the noble personage. In fact, the committee went much further, and recommended that beacons be established not only at Copper Point on Long Island, but also on Goat Island. Trinity House was quick to grant approval, and the Board of Trade awarded the building contract to a Mr Limerick. Unfortunately, Mr Limerick had bitten off more than he could chew, and insolvency forced him to retire from the project. So another Mr Limerick took over – the first Mr Limerick's brother. Exactly how the £1,129 paid by the board was divided between the brothers is not recorded, but one hopes it did not lead to a falling out!

In 1975, on the recommendation of the Inspecting Committee, various modifications were made to the beacon, including the construction of an access ladder up the side and the installation of an acetylene light. The light was not actually commissioned for another two years. Its character of one flash every 10 seconds complied with specifications provided by the International Association of Lighthouse Authorities which designated the beacon an 'east cardinal mark'. The colour scheme of yellow at the bottom, black in the middle, yellow at the top also indicated that the structure was an east cardinal mark. In plain language, approaching vessels knew that, for safety, it should be passed on the eastern side. A further indication of this was the east cardinal topmark – an emblem reiterating the necessity of passing on the eastern side. The installation of the topmark and the painting of yellow-black-yellow bands was not completed until 1980, and the paint had hardly dried when, just one year later and on the recommendation of the Inspector of Lights, the east cardinal mark at Copper Point graduated to lighthouse proper and was painted white. ✳ *Qfl (3) W 10s*

Crookhaven

Crookhaven lighthouse in Rock Island, at the entrance to the harbour of the same name, has been in existence for many years, and though an unmanned light, was the responsibility of the keepers who happened to be on rock leave from either Mizen or Fastnet. These men did not take too kindly to this shore duty, and were greatly relieved when a local attendant was appointed. The shore dwellings for the Mizen and Fastnet were based in Rock Island, about 1.5 miles from the village of Goleen. The little lighthouse within the compound is hardly noticeable, but Rock Island itself was always a hive of activity, as lighthouse personnel were forever on the move. The keepers' families were totally integrated into the local community, and many of our present-day lightkeepers went to school in Goleen. It was also well known as the 'Waterloo' for many a supernumerary sent down from Dublin to do duty. In those days of relief by boats and the ensuing 'overdues', keepers would be forced to spend many weeks 'walking around', and visiting the local hostelries became, all too often, habit forming. Money was always scarce, and the longer one spent ashore, the more devious were the methods devised for remaining solvent. I remember well on a fair day in Schull witnessing a rather unique sight. Two lightkeepers, one of them a principal keeper and both dressed in full regalia, were standing ankle deep in cow dung entertaining the passers-by. The principal keeper was giving a plaintive rendition of 'Noreen Bawn' on a battered old violin, while his assistant went around with the cap. They then changed places, and the assistant keeper sang 'Danny Boy' as the principal keeper collected. Very well they did too, and there was many a moist eye among the onlookers. Later that same night, at around 3 a.m., I was awakened in my quarters in the Valley (the name for our abode in Rock Island) by one of those same keepers, and invited to partake of half a dozen lobsters which had just been cooked. Not too far away was a lobster storage pond, and these delicious creatures were not too hard to come by. I might add that I was not myself averse to wading waist deep into the pool on a dark night and liberating the odd lobster or crayfish.

A great source of extra revenue for the keepers was the surplus coal which occasionally became available. The dwellings had an allotment of 7 tons of coal per house, and by careful manipulation of the supplies, a fairly substantial amount of coal could be saved and offered for sale. Sometimes, a barter system was operated, and many a keeper's house was kept replenished with a constant supply of potatoes and vegetables for favours rendered. The more extreme form of bartering was the supply of cast-off uniforms and caps to the locals. Being made of the best material available, they were much in demand; indeed, almost anywhere around the coast, but more especially on the islands, many a local head could be seen adorned by a lightkeeper's cap. I have an abiding memory of being on Tory Island some years ago and seeing a scarecrow, no less, fully decked out in a battered service uniform and cap. What a tale he could tell! The maintenance men's houses were also supplied with coal and oil, and this came at the very moderate charge of a shilling for a hundredweight of coal, and sixpence a gallon for the oil. This charge, however, was nominal, and used mainly for checking purposes.

Like all service houses on the coast, those at Rock Island were very well maintained, but it was left to the discretion of the occupants to adorn them as they wished. As the usual stay for most families was about three years, in most cases no great effort was made in this direction. When the keepers decided they would rather live in accommodation of their own choice, the houses at Rock Island were sold, and it was not long before the site took on a whole new appearance. I was down there some time ago, and was amazed at what time, effort and money could do to transform these rather drab dwellings into the most exquisite modern apartments.

The Fastnet Rock, about 9 miles straight out from Rock Island, is clearly visible most nights, and I am sure the ghost of many an old light-keeper must be floating around the compound, looking out at what must have been his lonely habitat for many long stints. Irish Lights still maintains a buoy yard at Rock Island, but nowadays I am afraid it is a case of 'tread softly, stranger'. *Lfl WR 8s*

Mizen Head

Just down the road from the picturesque village of Crookhaven is the Mizen Head – perhaps one of our better-known peninsulas. Over the years, the Mizen has witnessed drama at sea. During construction of the fog-signal station in 1908, the resident engineer and his workmen enacted a tremendous feat of rescue when they saved 63 people from the SS *Irada*, which was wrecked off the head on 22 December. The master of the vessel blamed the lack of a fog signal at Mizen for the disaster. Mizen again came to the rescue when, on 2 February 1940, the keepers and local people gave help to twelve crew members of the Norwegian trawler, *Songa*, which had been sunk by a German submarine. Half a century later, in 1986, the former Taoiseach – our prime minister – Mr Charles Haughey, and the crew of his yacht were very nearly lost in fog at the base of the cliff just under the lighthouse. But for the diligence of the

Mizen Head

lightkeeper on watch, a major tragedy could very easily have ensued. The keeper, while unable to effect a rescue himself, kept both the crew of the yacht and the rescuing craft aware of the situation at all times, and must have been a source of great consolation to the beleaguered yachtsmen. They were rescued eventually, after many freezing hours at sea, and complimented the lightkeepers on their valiant efforts.

The Mizen is rather unique in that the lighthouse there is only of recent origin. While sanction was given by the Board of Trade for a lighthouse and fog signal in 1906, it was decided that only the latter navigational aid was deemed necessary. A reinforced concrete bridge was built by Messrs Thome and Company in 1907. The bridge, designed by Mr M. Noel Ridley, was one of the first prefabricated structures built in the British Isles. It consists of two parabolic sections spanning 52 metres, and has a footway almost 46 metres above sea level. Dwellings were also built on-site.

Mizen Head was raided by armed men on 21 May 1920, and explosives intended for the fog signal were spirited away. As no protection was offered to the station by the government of the day, the Board decided to close down all the explosive-fog-signal stations around the coast. Mizen was re-established on 29 February 1924, and a wireless beacon installed in 1931. The lighthouse, a small tower that was not built until 1959, has a candela power of 21,000, and can be seen for 16 nautical miles in clear weather. * *Iso W 4s*

Fastnet

The date 24 October 1964 is firmly etched in my mind. I was sitting – or, to be precise, sprawled – in the cutter of the *Valonia* awaiting my turn to get astride a short piece of timber at the end of a rope, and trying desperately to remember the drill that would save me from being washed by a mad, green, rolling sea that was getting rougher by the minute. I have no hesitation in admitting that I was terrified, and when Big Patsy, the cox, yelled above the din, 'You're next,' it was only pure shame that got me slipping and sliding over the baskets of grub, the enormous oars, hopelessly entangled nets and innumerable feet encased in waist-high rubber boots. I had just reached the side of the gunwale when a mighty wave took the boat right across the concrete landing and ditched it in a deep trough on the other side. I could see that the experienced boatmen were shaken by this rare occurrence, and everything became totally confused. Way above, on top of the rocks, the keepers were at the main derrick, awaiting the sign from below to start winding up the rope. Big Patsy stood erect, aft in the boat, apparently oblivious to any danger, yet keeping a wary eye on the massive rollers that were coming with frightening regularity around the pier head of the rock. The commands and countermands were being shouted from all sides, but being very much in the Castletown idiom, I could not make out a word anyone was saying. Suddenly, I realised I was being propelled towards the short stick they call a bo'sun's chair, and before I knew it, I got a mighty heave over the side and was unexpectedly airborne. Then came the long, slow winch over boiling seas to a platform high up on the rock. The derrick was pulled in, willing hands helped me free myself of the chair, and I was standing, for the first time, on the Fastnet Rock. Over the years, that type of landing was enacted many times on various rocks around our coast, but that first trip to the Fastnet was, for me, the one I will always remember.

Actually, there were two lighthouses built on this rock. The decision to build the first one was taken after the wreck of an American ship, the *Stephen Whitney*, in November 1847 – a tragedy that cost a hundred lives. Although there was a light on Clear Island at the time, it was deemed to be too far inshore to be effective.

Two very eminent lighthouse builders of the nineteenth century, George Halpin and his son, are credited with having built well over 50 lighthouses. When George Halpin was given the task of building the new lighthouse on the Fastnet Rock, he opted to use cast iron. The plates were 25 millimetres thick, and encased a steel trunk to take the pendulum-like weight. The top of the lantern was 53 metres above low water, and the light first shone from the Fastnet in 1854. The keepers were housed in a separate dwelling, to the northeast of the tower. Dwellings were also built at Rock Island for the keepers and their families.

Although an excellent building, and with allowances made for all possible contingencies, it quickly became apparent that this iron tower would eventually suffer the same fate as the Calf lighthouse (of which more later). But for the existence of a nearby rock – the Little Fastnet, which lies to the south of the main road and takes the brunt of those massive seas – this lighthouse would have, in all probability, been carried away. As it happened, the lantern was badly damaged in the same gale that destroyed the Calf, and it was decided that the very important position of this rock merited the best possible structure. While the original lighthouse was built on the summit of the rock, it was proposed to start the foundation for its replacement at a much lower level.

The building of the present Fastnet was in every way a most remarkable achievement. I have often thought it a pity that such a structure could not have been built on our shoreline so that its streamlined beauty could be appreciated by more people. The lower part of the lighthouse is well below sea level, and steps were cut into the side of the rock to receive the partial courses necessary for this operation. The granite stones were dressed and shaped in the yards of Messrs John Freeman and Sons, of Penrhyn in Cornwall, and each stone was dovetailed and cemented to those above and below it. Each part of the tower was first erected in Cornwall, and it can be said that this particular lighthouse was built twice over. When satisfaction with one part of the tower was achieved, it was dispatched to a prepared site at Rock Island, while the top course of each section was retained at the works to form the bottom course of the next section.

Rock Island became a very busy place for the duration of the Fastnet project. Extra houses were built, as was a barracks for the workmen. The pier was improved considerably, and a crane and even a tramway were installed. There was also a masonry store and magazines for housing the explosives. All these improvements to the shore station paid handsome dividends, as it was used as a buoy depot for many years afterwards.

The weather was unkind during the building of the Fastnet, and it was not until August 1899 that the first solid course was laid on the rock. Douglass, the original engineer, retired from the scene at this point due to ill health, but all credit must be given to him for designing virtually everything connected with the lighthouse, though not the lantern and optics. On the retirement of Douglass, the project was taken in hand by a Mr C.W. Scott, who was appointed engineer to the Board. As for the workmen on the rock, no dedicated body of men ever worked so hard and in such extreme conditions to achieve the completion of this fine lighthouse. The foreman mason, James Kavanagh, hardly saw the shore between 1896 and 1903. This was by choice, though he did eventually have to come ashore when he became ill. Ironically, he died not long afterwards. It was a great tragedy, as this man was largely responsible for the extraordinary workmanship that went into every aspect of the tower. He was a hard taskmaster, and the men had to rise at 5 a.m. every morning, and were expected to first thoroughly wash themselves and their quarters. Accommodation was very limited, and it is said the men had to sleep three to a bunk, though the foreman had his own quarters. Accidents appear to have been few, but two men each lost an eye and another broke a leg.

Despite the unusually bad weather, work progressed at a fairly rapid rate, and four years after commencement – in the middle of the summer of 1903 – the last masonry course, number 89, was laid. The tower was now ready for the optic. The Commissioners decided on a biform light as the most suitable and reliable apparatus. The lantern consisted of two four-sided lenses, one on top of the other, and was made by Messrs Chance Brothers Ltd., of Smethwick in England. This double lens had a twofold objective in that the light gave a much wider arc, and should any mishap befall one burner, the other would still be in operation. As in most of the larger lighthouses, the lanterns are floated on mercury baths to ensure the least friction and to allow the character of the light to be set and maintained accurately. In 1904, the light was first exhibited from the new tower. Shortly afterwards, the old iron tower was partially dismantled, though the lower part was kept for use as an oil stove.

The cost of building the Fastnet lighthouse came to something in the region of £70,000. This included £10,000 for the construction of a ship specifically for the operation – the *Ierne*, built in 1898 in Glasgow. On completion of the Fastnet, the *Ierne* replaced the *Moya* as the attendant vessel for the south-west coast, and remained active in the service until 1954, when she was replaced by a ship of the same name.

During my many visits to the Fastnet, I have marvelled at the courage, ingenuity and endurance of the men who built this tower with every possible concession to authentic subtleties, and which was technically way ahead of its time. There are two balconies – one outside the service room and the other around the lantern. I have stood on the latter, which is 50 metres high, and watched a mighty sea climb up the tower as if some giant hands were intent on pushing it right over the lantern. On bright sunny days, when the seas were in turmoil, the myriad of colours cascading through the endless foam could hold one spellbound for hours.

I learnt many things during my regular visits to the Fastnet, but perhaps the most rewarding and enduring was the ability to live in isolation with my fellow man. Lightkeepers have always struck me as being the very essence of tolerance and understanding, and while I have witnessed a few minor feuds, I believe, on the whole, they have learnt the true value of the idiom, 'Take plenty of no notice'. The Fastnet is one of the very few lighthouses where one has to live in the actual tower, and consequently that feeling of 'togetherness' is more realistic than at other stations. In bad weather, the tower becomes something of a tomb, and I have experienced as many as four to five weeks when neither the storm shutters nor the massive iron entrance door would be opened. It was at times like these that the true nature of the lightkeeper was put to the test, and in pre-television times – when endless days of isolation had utterly exhausted every topic of conversation and boredom weighed heavily on each man – the real lightkeeper surfaced. What an endurance test it must be to spend week after week, month after month, and even year after year, literally locked up in places like the Fastnet. In Ireland, even in the sunny south, winters can be very long indeed, and as if that was not bad enough, imagine having to suffer the same two human beings for all that time. No wonder people like myself were always welcomed, if only as a new face. In that respect, I consider myself extremely lucky, as I was always the visitor, never the resident.

For exercise during those enforced sojourns, endless journeys would be made across the service-room floor, each man going in opposite directions. When I became the fourth man, things tended to become a little crowded and it was necessary to take the exercise in turns; what one would have given at times like these for a little jogging space. During these 'walks', a diversion would often be provided by a pet seagull that would peer inquisitively through the thick storm glass, no doubt wondering what was preventing those mad, marching lunatics inside the tower from feeding him. He would eventually go away, only to return when he once again saw a plate of grub on the window ledge.

Amazingly enough, the time on the Fastnet passed quite quickly. No one seems to have an explanation for this, but when the weather eventually moderated and one could get out and about, the rock took on a whole new dimension. After a bad storm, hundreds of dead birds are to be found lying around the tower balconies, especially on lighthouses such as Tuskar and Fastnet. These birds are blinded by the powerful beams of light, and crash into the windows. They come in all shapes and sizes, and many a good feed of blackbird pie could be had after one of these storms. For some strange reason, not nearly as many birds are killed in this fashion nowadays, although in the majority of lighthouses the power of the light has been greatly increased.

Fishing off the Fastnet is possibly the best on the coast, although a weighted heaving line has to be used to achieve the distance. Enormous pollock are always readily available, and I believe this fish must be the most prolific around the coast as I have rarely seen any other species caught. I did, however, see a giant skate foul-hooked by a local workman on Inishtrahull, but just as he was about to pull it up over the cliff it slipped off and floated away on the tide. It was quite understandable that the unfortunate fisherman shed copious tears at his loss, especially since we all seemed to be living full-time on a diet of pollock.

The Fastnet must be one of the warmest rocks on the coast, and when the weather was fine, the long, tedious days spent on the tower were soon forgotten and the outdoor life enjoyed to the full. No one ever left the station without having acquired a healthy tan, and I can recall shaving off a beard I had grown during a particularly hot spell of weather, forgetting completely that the skin underneath would be snow white. I came home looking like a piebald, and remained that way for some weeks afterwards.

Summers on the rock were all too short, and even the advent of the helicopter reliefs did little to lessen the hardship on such stations. Overdues were the bane of lightkeepers' lives, and these stations had more than their share of them. Even the helicopter reliefs failed to wipe out this constant menace, as high winds and fog are a permanent feature of Irish weather.

I dare say the Fastnet will always be held in awe by the service. Together with Blackrock, Mayo (Mayo is used to distinguish it from Blackrock, Sligo), the Maidens and Eagle Island, the Fastnet was always known in the service as a 'punishment station'. If any keeper stepped out of line or committed some serious indiscretion, he was sure to be sent to one of these stations. Mind you, not all the keepers at those stations were sent there for indiscretions committed, and here I would like to pay tribute to a particular lightkeeper friend who spent almost nine years on the Fastnet – mostly by choice. I first met him many years ago in the Loop Head lighthouse in County Clare on one of my earliest trips to that coast. I arrived by bus in the little village of Kilbaha on a bitterly cold November night, and having failed to locate a taxi to transport me the remaining 3 miles to the lighthouse, a kindly farmer I met in the local pub offered to take me there by horse and cart. Sitting on the side of the cart – the intense cold permeating my whole body – I made futile attempts to extricate my brand new overcoat from the grease between the shaft and wheel of the cart. Before long, I was beginning to have serious doubts as to the romantic nature of this lighthouse world. The clatter of the cart in the lighthouse yard was heard inside the dwellings, and brought forth an amazing sight. This enormous, bull-like, wild-haired man, dressed only in dirty pants with a shirt opened down to the waist – exposing a massive barrel of a chest – came forward and lifted me bodily from the cart. 'Welcome to Loop Head,' said Mr M.J. Crowley. I had met 'Pa'.

It took me quite a while to adjust to my surroundings, but more especially to Pa. It is practically impossible to describe on paper the way he had of expressing himself. If you can imagine trying to decipher a passage of Joyce's *Ulysses*, punctuated by a garbled miscellany of monosyllables, you will have some idea of what it was like. His appearance matched his vocabulary, and his expressions ranged between those of a fearsome-looking pirate and a benign polar bear. Pa had spent some of his early days at sea, and his descriptions of the cavorting hula girls around the South Seas were hilarious. Although it must have been many years since he had been a sailor, he could still recount vividly the various attributes of those lovely ladies. Every now and then, though, he would remember who he was describing them to (I was still very young), and then that wild, savage look would appear, and God help any of those unfortunate hula girls who happened to be near to hand. A massive fist would come crashing down on the nearest object, and the poor girl whom he was loving a minute ago would now be dismembered.

At that time, Pa was very interested in guns, and kept a small arsenal in the kitchen. He seemed to be forever cleaning and oiling these guns. My room was directly over the kitchen, and I was sharing it with a Mr Martin McCarthy, a coast tradesman, now sadly deceased. I remarked one day to Martin how Pa had a habit of leaving these guns pointed towards the ceiling, and I wondered what would happen if by accident one of them was loaded. Although the remark was only intended as a joke, we were not long moving our beds to a safer position overhead.

Pa also had a motorbike at that time, and offered to show me some of the sights. We set off one Sunday afternoon, and it was one I will never forget. He mustn't have had the bike taxed, as he kept to all the by-roads. In those days, they were in some state, with potholes a foot deep. Pa was going that fast, we were airborne most of the time. He kept shouting back to me, pointing to some interesting object with one hand and trying to steer the bike with the other. I was too frightened to look either way, and clung onto him for dear life. Ducks, hens and even cattle were treated with disdain, and had there been a speed limit, we would have both wound up in jail. Pa never stopped once, and we arrived back in the lighthouse some hours later. I was unable to sit down for a week.

After leaving Loop Head, I did not meet Pa again for almost ten years. I was dangling on a rope over mountainous seas at the Fastnet Rock, too terrified to move a muscle, and I knew of only one man who would dare bring out the steamer on a day like that. Yes, my friend Pa was right there on the landing, ready to grab me in those massive arms. There is no doubt but Pa loved the Fastnet. If ever a rock was built to suit a light-keeper, this was Pa's rock. As I have said, he spent years on it, and other lightkeepers must have been eternally grateful to him. He rarely failed to come down singing in the morning, and the more the tower shook with those tremendous seas, the more he revelled in it. I spent a few months with him there and he treated me like an honoured guest. Water and coal had to be dragged up from the bottom of the tower, but whenever I went to do my share of the chores, Pa would have one of his assistants do it for me. Whether he thought me incapable or whether he had it in for one of the keepers, I was never quite sure.

A powerful swimmer, Pa would swim miles off the rock. Often, he would disappear, and we would be sure he had gone for good. But then a big roar would come floating across the water, and we would see him tossing and tumbling like a giant porpoise. He used to anchor a buoy a little way off the rock for my convenience, and that was as far as I would venture. A bit of swell got up one day when I was in the water, and Pa came out to me. I grabbed him around the neck and nearly drowned both of us getting back. He swam way out to a trawler another day, and dragged a 12-foot eel back to the rock. He cut steaks off the eel, put them on the pan and covered them with onions. At first reluctant to partake of this unappetising-looking meal, I was eventually persuaded, and I can heartily recommend them to the uninitiated.

Although essentially a non-smoker and non-drinker, Pa would sometimes give me a cigarette at night. I would return the compliment the following night, and after a while this became something of a ritual. He never seemed to need or ask for anything from the Commissioners, and he must have saved them a lot of expense during his time on the Fastnet. I remember one threadbare dishcloth being used for the whole of my time there. I sometimes think he could have run that rock without any aid from the service. I wonder what he would say if he saw it now, with its central heating and helipad, not to mention the electric toilet. I doubt if he would take kindly to these changes. The 'old' Fastnet was Pa's rock, and he would not have had it any other way.

When ashore, Pa lived in one of the service dwellings at Rock Island. I met him there many times, and we would swap yarns about the Fastnet, which he could see quite plainly from his back door. He was a very religious man, and though unmarried had a great love of children. He would fill his pockets with sweets from the village, and share them amongst the children at the dwellings. I often noticed a wistful look coming into his eyes then, no doubt remembering and regretting.

On one of those occasions when I was going ashore from the Fastnet, Pa brought out the steamer on another bad day. We could not use the derrick as there was too much wind, so his plan was for me to jump into the cutter on the lee side of the rock. He tied a rope around me and told me when to jump. I jumped all right, but Pa forgot to let go of the rope, and I landed up to my neck in the water. When I was dragged into the boat, I looked back and there was Pa doing a sort of war dance on the rock, his arm torn after being dashed by a wave against a rock. But he was in high spirits, having proven once again that he could beat the elements. He was wrong, of course, but then his luck had not deserted him as yet.

One of the first Christmas cards issued by the service featured the Fastnet, and I duly sent one to Pa. He thanked me most profusely in a multi-page letter which was almost completely illegible. I sent him one every year after that, and got similar letters of thanks. The last place I saw Pa was at the Hook. His strength had drained away, the brown was gone from his face, the mouth had lost its ready grin and the sharp eyes were dull and full of pain. Yes, those elements he thought he had mastered long ago on the Fastnet had finally taken their toll. His worry, though, was not about death, but about life; he wasn't doing anything. His battles with the elements were over. Here, he could literally walk away from the weather. I tried to talk cheerfully, and he tried to respond, but after a few seconds, we lapsed into a strained silence. I think we both knew we were pretending, and the pretence was proving too much for us.

Many keepers saw service with Pa Crowley, some possibly to their detriment. I know he was not the easiest of men to get on with, and took a lot of understanding. I never had to spend long periods with him, and can only judge him on those short acquaintances. He was a kindly man to me, and a good, if somewhat unusual, friend. He will, of course, remain what had always been my preconceived idea of a lightkeeper.
✱ *Fl W 5s*

West Coast ✵

Sheep's Head

The secret of our south-western peninsulas lies in their inaccessibility. Perhaps EU-financed bridges will one day connect these remote outposts, but until then these peninsulas will intrigue and entice the traveller, inviting us to investigate their mysteries. Few can match the beauty of Sheep's Head at the southern tip of Bantry Bay, and those in the service of Irish Lights have good reason to traverse its narrow roads, for at its extremity can be found a lighthouse not yet 40 years old. The construction of the ill-fated oil terminal at Whiddy Island, adjacent to the town of Bantry, and the arrival on the scene of oil tankers necessitated the erection of a lighthouse. Modelled on what at that time was the three-year-old lighthouse on Achillbeg, Sheep's Head light came into service on 14 October 1968.

As was so often the case in the history of Irish Lights, construction of the tower at Sheep's Head was a logistical nightmare. As no road led to the site, building materials and lighthouse equipment had to be airlifted by helicopter from nearby Kilcrohane. In all, around 250 lifts were required. The round tower atop a square building stands 7 metres high, its lantern 83 metres above the sea. Its light is divided into white and red sectors, the red sector warning approaching vessels of the submerged South Bullig rocks. At 59,000 candelas, the white sector has a range of 19 nautical miles, while the filters in the red sector reduce its range to 15 nautical miles.

The lighthouse came to life just as automation was getting underway, and its operation was monitored from afar by the keepers at Mizen Head through a UHF radio link. Now, in common with all our lights, Sheep's Head is monitored by the control centre in faraway Dún Laoghaire.

✳ Fl (3) WR 15s

Roancarrig

When a man signed up for a lighthouse life, he signed his family up, too. Usually, children were still to come, but when they did, their existence was as much conditioned by the vagaries of this unusual occupation as was their father's. Tucks Tweedy, writing in *Beam*, the magazine of Irish Lights, noted one effect on children of life in the service.

> On their first days in school they could be seen on their own at break time, in one corner of the playground. However, as children are adaptable, they would soon integrate. Years later I asked a principal keeper, whose father had been stationed around the coast, how he had been affected by these moves. He told me of one instance when his family transferred from Roancarrig to Inishowen. Having spent six years listening to the West Cork dialect, on arriving in Donegal they found not only could they not understand Irish but English sounded foreign to them as well.

Roancarrig

From the air, Roancarrig is nothing more than a barren rock with a lighthouse. A ground-level inspection confirms this impression. Located at the eastern entrance to Bantry Bay, this flat-topped island – a mere 6 metres high – has been home to a lighthouse since 1847. The white tower, painted with a black band, bears the stamp of George Halpin, designer of this and so many other lighthouses in Ireland.

The necessity of a lighthouse here was made obvious by the many maritime calamities in the area, but the establishment of a light did not guarantee against further mishap. In recent years, a number of Spanish trawlers have come to grief on the rock. In 1972, the desperate crewmen of the *Josefa Lopez* scrambled to safety after their vessel sunk after striking Roancarrig. One of the unfortunate men died later of injuries. In 1990, the *Garadossa* lost power during a severe gale and was driven onto Roancarrig near the lighthouse. The captain and fourteen crewmen were brought to safety by helicopter, but a sailor from the Irish naval vessel, LE *Deirdre*, named Michael Quinn, was lost during the rescue operation.

Automation has not entirely eliminated the dangers associated with rock stations, as this recent report from the *Irish Examiner* illustrates:

> An employee of Irish Lights with suspected cardiac difficulties was evacuated from a lighthouse off West Cork this morning. Castletownbere lifeboat responded to a call to a man in his early thirties who had been working on the Roancarrig Lighthouse . . . Sea conditions were moderate with a two-metre swell, a force four wind and poor visibility . . . the lifeboat was unable to go alongside the landing pier at Roancarrig, and therefore the lifeboat launched its Y Boat – a small inflatable dingy . . . Two lifeboat crew landed on the Roancarrig and attended to the casualty . . .

Such are the hazards of ensuring 'the safety of all at sea'. ✸*Fl WR 3s*

Castletownbere

On our way west, let us pause in Castletownberehaven, which, as far as I know, has the second-longest place name in Ireland. For the purpose of this narrative, the shortened 'Castletown' is sufficient, as the full name is rarely used. The lighthouse here is of recent vintage – 1965 – and stands a mere 6 metres high. But sometimes that's all it takes.

Dwellings were built in Castletown for the lightkeepers of Roancarrig, but since the rock became automated, these dwellings have been used as holiday homes for service personnel. There are similar facilities at Ballycotton and Inishowen in Donegal. Near the dwellings at Castletown is the helicopter base from which all the south-west-coast lighthouses were relieved; indeed, once every two weeks, the place is still very busy, as all the lighthouses have still to be maintained by service personnel.

I know the town better than most, as I have spent many weary days there, trying to get to the Fastnet, Bull and the like. My record overdue spent there was about five weeks, during which I walked endless roads and hoped desperately for an improvement in the weather to enable the relief to be carried out. While Castletown is situated amid the most beautiful scenery in the country, and its inhabitants the most friendly and obliging, I have built up a pathological dread of ever being stranded in that town again. The helipad is some way outside the town on the Cork side and, having come ashore from any of the rocks, I would not venture to town under any pretence, choosing instead to head straight for Cork and home. While overdues nowadays are rare occurrences – thanks to the excellent helicopter services – they can still occur. Many a planned overnight stay turned out to be one of several days due to prolonged gale-force conditions. ✱*Dir Oc WRG 5s*

Ardnakinna

The light at Ardnakinna has a chequered history. Located on the west point of Bere Island, it originally came into service as a beacon in 1850 at the behest of the Admiralty, its supervision entrusted to a local man. When in 1901 the Admiralty designated the adjacent Castletownbere a dockyard, the Board of Trade agreed to the Admiralty's request that responsibility for the beacon and buoys be entrusted to the navy men. Irish independence in 1922 had many unforeseen consequences, including the discontinuance of the beacon at Ardnakinna. The stranding of a trawler near Castletownbere in 1945 prompted locals to seek the restoration of the beacon, but there followed years of official procrastination. Reports and recommendations went unheeded until 1964, when approval was finally granted for the conversion of Ardnakinna beacon to a lighthouse.

The original structure stood 50 feet high, and conversion essentially meant adding a lantern to the round white tower, thus raising its height to 66 feet. A lantern that had previously been in service aboard a lightvessel was modified and installed at Ardnakinna. Established on 23 November 1965, its character of two white and red flashes every 10 seconds has a range of 17 nautical miles for the white sector, and 14 nautical miles for the red. ✳*Fl (2) WR 10s* ✳

Bull Rock

Of the five lighthouses on the south-western part of our coast, one could say that the Fastnet and the Skelligs are the best known. Though their companions – the Bull Rock, Inishtearaght and Roancarrig – are relatively anonymous, I feel I must give pride of place to Bull Rock, as it was instrumental in having me barred – almost – for the only time in my life from what we know as a 'licensed premises'. Lightkeepers, tradesmen, technical and maintenance staff are forever either going to or coming off lighthouses, and when their paths cross, the conversation usually centres around the various difficulties which inevitably ensue. I was on my way to the Bull Rock and happened to be staying in the same hotel as a lightkeeper who was on his way to the Maidens lighthouse, off the coast of Antrim. In time-honoured tradition, we agreed to meet for a few drinks in the lounge of our rather grand hotel. The night prior to reliefs always seemed to warrant those few extra drinks, as one was very conscious of the abstemious month ahead. Anyway, our conversation centred on the various attributes of the lighthouses to which we were both going, and I asserted that, while I always enjoyed being on the Bull, the Maidens did nothing at all for me. My friend countered by saying that while being on the Bull might be more pleasant, coming off the Maidens was a lot easier and entailed very little exertion. The conversation continued in this vein for some time, and perhaps because of the potent beverage we were both enjoying, our voices became somewhat animated. It was then we noticed two old ladies looking at us in a rather strange manner. Very soon, they were deep in conversation with the manager, and it was not long before he approached us and requested we leave immediately as the two ladies objected very strongly to the spicy tone of our conversation. It took us quite some time to convince him that we were simply discussing lighthouses. To his credit and that of the two old dears, when the situation was eventually resolved, drinks were on the house and a memorable night was had by all. I think they even believed half the lies we told them.

The Bull Rock is the largest of a group of rocks known as the Bull, Cow, Calf and Heifer. I know of no logical reason for such names, as the resemblance to any of these noble beasts is purely contrived. The

Calf has the distinction of being the first of these rocks to have been graced by a lighthouse, the Bull having been considered at that time to be too high for such a project. But the elements soon played a major part in the ultimate and permanent location of the lighthouse.

The tower on the Calf was one of the few iron lighthouses built in Ireland around the middle of the nineteenth century – that period which is generally accepted as the Industrial Age. Built in 1866, it was soon apparent that the materials used were totally unsuited to this unusually vulnerable lighthouse. The constant pounding of the tower by the sea loosened some of the bolts securing the cast-iron plates, and caused concern about the stability of the tower. In addition, part of the balcony and retaining rail were washed away. The tower was strengthened in 1870 by adding an iron skirt around the bottom two storeys. Despite the herculean efforts made to strengthen the tower, however, the lighthouse actually broke in half – above the reinforcing – in 1881. Miraculously, no loss of life occurred, as the keepers had portents of the impending disaster. A temporary light was erected on Dursey Island in February 1822 while the new tower and station were being constructed on the Bull. The island is a massive 100 metres above sea level, is practically circular in shape and has a diameter of some 200 metres. Being at such a high level, towers such as the Bull – while built to withstand the elements in all their fury – do not require the same durable measures as, say, the Fastnet. This lighthouse exhibits an impressive 4.5 million candelas, the light visible for some 31 nautical miles. ✱ *Fl W 15s*

Skelligs

Skellig Michael, on which the Skelligs lighthouse is built, has long been the subject of books and tourist guides, along with its counterpart, Little

Skellig. To add to that body of work, here is an account of not one, but two lighthouses on Skellig Michael. Great Skellig – as it is more commonly known – is a 120-metres-high pyramidal mass of sandstone, loose slate and crumbling rock, and lies about 8 miles west of Bolus Head in Kerry.

The upper of the two original lighthouses was constructed at 115 metres above sea level – not many of our lighthouses are built at such a height. That intrepid lighthouse builder, George Halpin, was the architect for the two towers erected on the Skelligs. The Corporation for Preserving and Improving the Port of Dublin, which acquired the island in 1820, felt that two lighthouses were necessary because of the peculiar layout of the island. So, at heights of 115 metres and 55 metres, the two lighthouses were erected. At the upper site, a fog-signal station was also established. The lighthouses were neither remarkable in design nor in structure, as it was believed their sheltered positions would offer protection from the elements. The upper light was discontinued as early as 1866, but the lower light is still functioning, though the present tower replaced the old one in 1966.

I was practically a resident on the island during the building of the new station. As many as sixteen men were housed in hastily erected quarters, and it was certainly not luxurious living by any standards. Whether by accident or design, a copy of a book on the building of the Fastnet had been strategically 'abandoned' by some former 'inmate', and became almost required reading. Compared to what Mr Kavanagh and his merry men had to put up with when constructing the Fastnet, our conditions could not be described as primitive. We also had fun, most of it at the expense of each other. The keepers always kept a few hens on the Skelligs, and due to the peculiar feeding matter around the rock, the eggs had deep-red yokes. These were really delicious, but always very scarce, and during that period, a constant vigil was mounted by one or other of the keepers. But when an opportunity presented itself, I replaced a few of the eggs with my own insipid variety. Shortly after, I spied a none-too-bright keeper unsuspectingly gather the replacement eggs. Walking slowly back to the quarters, he examined the eggs reflectively. Though he said nothing to the others, he may have often thought later what wonderful hens they were that they could lay eggs already code marked! All eggs sold commercially had to have a code mark in those days.

Life for fowl on the Skelligs was often precarious, as a fair number were lost over the cliffs. When trying to fly down from the heights to the lighthouse road, they often overran the retaining wall, landed hundreds of metres down below on the rocks, and eventually wound up in the sea. There, they could be seen for days afterwards, floundering about, and it was rather sad that no help could be extended to these unfortunate creatures.

Oddly enough, since the helipad was built, landing by helicopter on the Skelligs has become much more difficult due to the landing pad being positioned too near the overhanging cliff. The original site for the pad was supposed to be at the 'Wailing Woman', but local superstition played a major role in its abandonment.

The Skelligs was never my favourite; indeed, in summer, when the hordes of visitors invade the place, it is difficult to imagine one is actually on a lighthouse at all. The dwellings face west, and for most of the time are in the shadow of the cliff wall. Consequently, a bleakness permeates the place, and the ever-trickling rivulets result in a permanently damp terrain. What made it attractive to the keepers – even before the advent of the helicopter – was the reliability of reliefs. The landing is in a very sheltered position, and boats from Valentia, Cahirciveen and Derrynane arrive daily during the summer. In the old days, the captain of the lighthouse tender would always endeavour to keep both the Skelligs and Tearaght reliefs together, as it was quite a journey from

Castletown and these two rocks are close neighbours. But as we prepared to go ashore for Christmas during the building of the new Skelligs tower, we became very anxious. Though we had perfectly good landings, the Tearaght had none, and the tender was making no move to relieve us. Eventually, after threatening to order a boat from Valentia, the captain relented and we all arrived back in Castletown the day before Christmas Eve. As we were late in, we had to stay the night, so our first stop after collecting our mail was at John Dennehy's pub. John had been the building foreman on the Skelligs job, so this was our obvious halt. The first round called for was fourteen 'half-ones', and every man called his turn after that. Even the non-imbibers felt they were entitled to partake. It turned out to be quite a session, but we were a sorry-looking bunch on the rickety bus to Cork the next morning.

In those days, wages were diligently posted in cash every week to the local post office, and after a few months on a rock, counting the contents of those registered letters was a pleasant chore. One really felt like a millionaire, and tended to forget that 24 hours a day every day went into the acquisition of same.

Something that has always intrigued me is the small proportion of Irish people who visit the Skelligs. I encountered nationalities of all kinds over the years, but very few of our own would appear to have even a passing interest in what must surely be considered one of our greatest natural phenomena. Personally, I have never tired of climbing those 600 steps to the beehive huts and marvelling at the anchorite life those monks of the early Celtic Church must have led. I have an abiding memory of a little Scottish priest who came out with a party to say Mass at the summit. Unfortunately, a fog came down, and Mass had to be said in our quarters instead. A very jolly nun – a sister of former Kerry star footballer, Mick O'Connell – was among the party. The priest's homily on the origin, piety, dedication and hardships of the Skelligs monks surpassed anything

I have heard or read since. We were all so enthralled that no one noticed the change in the weather, and when we went down to the landing, the boat had pulled out from the pier to avoid being damaged. As there were twenty visitors, things began to look ominous. But we all chipped in and prepared a meal of sorts for them. Fortunately, the weather abated somewhat, and though it was now dark, we managed to get them all safely back onto the boat. In the meantime, they had made a collection for the grub they had consumed, and this we invested in Sweeps tickets. But our prayers seemed not to impress the Almighty, because all of us still needed to be in gainful employment for a long time afterwards.

Before leaving the Skelligs, I must pay tribute to the three lightkeepers who withstood the fierce southerly gale of 27 December 1955, when an enormous sea almost washed the lantern away. The light was put out, and one of the keepers in the lantern was slightly injured. At a height of 55 metres, it must have been a frightening night. I happened to be one of the men sent down to effect repairs to the incandescent plant, and having spent eight days on Valentia Island (the reliefs were made from there), we eventually landed on the rock. The damage was shocking. The road from the landing up to the fog-signal hut 115 metres above was torn up, and the cliffs had dislodged tons of rubble, making a passage to the quarters almost impossible. But it is an ill wind that does not do someone some good. D3s – extra-curricular payments for work performed outside normal duties – were very much in evidence for a long time after, and I remember a keeper throwing just one shovelful of rubble over the cliff every day – no doubt to keep his conscience clear. The keepers were not the only culprits in this department, as in my case – due to an error in my work sheet – it was remarked caustically that the Skelligs was unique in having a 26-hour working day.

Another beneficial result of that storm was that the fog signal was closed down for good. This must surely have been in answer to some keeper's prayers, because having to stay alone for 4 hours at a time in the firing hut was quite an endurance. The fog-signal hut was built more than 60 metres above the main dwelling, and was cold, damp and very eerie. Undertaking the journey to the hut at night time could be hazardous, as falling stones and night-flying birds, such as the Manx shearwater, could make it really scary. Cut off totally, in fog, from his shipmates, and surrounded by the ghosts of its former inhabitants, many of the keepers must have kept a very lonely vigil firing those intolerable rockets.

It is hard to imagine that not too long ago, entire families lived on places like the Skelligs and the Tearaght. They were even transferred from one station to the other without ever coming ashore. What their lifestyle, fears and aspirations were must surely be pure conjecture. These families were effectively owned, body and soul, by the Commissioners of the day, and their every movement monitored for future reference. A sad reflection on those harsh times is the presence of two small graves that became the last resting place for two of the keepers' children. ✳ *Fl (3) W 10s*

Valentia

Situated at the western end of the Iveragh Peninsula, Valentia is an oblong island, roughly 7 miles long and 2 miles wide. Though small, history has not passed it by. The island – accessible by bridge since 1970 – is said to be home to the most westerly settled community in Europe, evidence of which lies in the prehistoric system of fields in bogland. Archaeological antiquities litter the island in the form of standing stones, cairns, wedge tombs and the remains of beehive huts. Slate was exported from the island, some of it finding its way onto the roof of the Palace of Westminster in London, and it's said that the Public Records Office in London utilises 25 miles of shelving composed of Valentia slate.

This small island made international news when the first transatlantic cable came ashore in 1865. Suddenly, this impoverished Irish-speaking community found itself at the centre of the technological revolution. From Newfoundland came the first message: 'Ship to shore. I have much pleasure in speaking to you through the 1865 cable.' Local people joined the crowd of dignitaries to celebrate this momentous occasion, and a perceptive reporter from the *Daily Telegraph* described the scene thus:

> It was a strange crowd to look at – half the men were barefoot, and none of them were decently clad; but all of them, I suppose, could have conversed in two languages; and the chances are that three or four could have seen the point of a joke, and given a smart answer themselves.

The Commissioners maintain three lights on Valentia Island – two of them are leading lights that work in conjunction with the main lighthouse at Cromwell Point, at the point of entry to the harbour. The leading lights were both constructed as beacons in 1891, and lights were established in both during the year of 1913. The rear light was discontinued in 1967, but re-established a decade later in 1977.

A block of eight shore dwellings for the keepers and families of Skelligs and Inishtearaght were built on the island at the turn of the century by Mr W.H. Jones of Dunmanway at a cost of £7,570. The keepers and their families took up residence in 1901, and both Skellig and Tearaght became relieving from Valentia – that is, the families left and only the lightkeepers remained, serving for a couple of weeks before being relieved.

✳*Front: Oc WRG 4s · Rear: Oc W 4s*

Cromwell Point

The lighthouse at Cromwell was first applied for by the Right Honourable Maurice Fitzgerald, Knight of Kerry, in 1828, but it was not until 1837, at the insistence of Mr Maurice O'Connell, that the building of the lighthouse was sanctioned. George Halpin was again the architect, and it was built by the Board's workmen for a little under £11,000. The tower – of cut stone and painted white – had a candela of a mere 2,000, and is only 17 metres above high water. The light was first exhibited on 1 February 1841. On 4 November 1947, when the light became unwatched, an acetylene generator was installed, and Mr Harry Staniford was appointed as attendant. Small, squat and mahogany-faced, this same man was one of the keepers on the Skelligs the night of the big storm. Harry was a good friend of mine, so I could never bring myself to point out to him his somewhat unusual comment when making his monthly returns to the office. His task was to charge the gas generators and make sure there were no leaks. For years, Harry's famous remark was remembered: 'Tested for leaks and found all leaks correct.' He would not have much trouble with his leaks today, as the light was electrified in 1966, and the candela increased to 34,500.

While I have very happy memories of the times I visited the island, I think it can honestly be said that it would not be among my favourites. Indeed, I have always maintained that the dirt road through Glenleam Wood, on the way to Cromwell lighthouse, is its most attractive feature. And I swear it has absolutely nothing to do with the fact that I courted many a fine Valentia lass on that very same road! However, Valentia can boast a remarkably mild climate, served as it is by the Gulf Stream, and that road to the lighthouse must be one of the most consistently warm walks anywhere in the country. When, many years ago, I witnessed snow on Valentia, it was uncharacteristic. It was a bad winter nationwide, and snow fell on the island for the first time in 23 years. Many of the adult population had never before seen snow, and the children were naturally enthralled.

When the lighthouse dwellings were sold and the lighthouse tender moved its base to Castletown, the loss to the island, both economically and socially, was enormous. Few islands can withstand an exodus such as this, and when finally the cable station went, the writing appeared to be on the wall. But with the advent of the bridge at Port Magee, a new lease of life was given to the island. ✳ *Fl WR 2s*

Inishtearaght

I suppose if I had to choose to live on any rock lighthouse, it would have to be Inishtearaght – commonly known as the 'Tearaght'. It must be all of 35 years since I first landed on this magical island. All I saw then was one huge mass of crumbling rock, inhabited by three lightkeepers, a few goats and thousands of rabbits. I wondered if I was going off my head to be out on this desolate outpost of civilisation, and was there nothing better to do in this life. On what was to be my last day there, seven years ago, I sat early one morning outside my quarters on that same rock. The sun poured down, with not a breath of wind; nothing moved, and only the cries of the guillemots, razorbills and fulmars interrupted the silence. Even the distinctive laughable chatter of the puffins seemed muffled. Far down the cliffs, a gentle sea lapped at the mouth of the cave, as it had done for centuries. Peace and tranquillity reigned and time stood still. I closed my eyes and lay back, coffee and toast forgotten. I thought, this is probably as near to heaven as I will ever get. All lighthouse people have their preference for the various rocks they visit, but I believe the early morning atmosphere becomes a deciding factor. The dwellings on Tearaght face directly east, and from early morning, there is an uninterrupted brightness which seems to continue right through the winter – no doubt due to its hyper-maritime climate.

The island is made up of two masses of rocky land, joined by another natural rock bridge some 75 metres above sea level. Originally named Brazil and Green Island, the latter rises to a height of 180 metres. During the building of the lighthouse, one of the workers was killed while collecting birds' eggs, and in 1913, Assistant Keeper Morgan slipped to his death near the east landing whilst herding milking goats; where he fell has since been called Morgan's Cove. There were also two remarkable escapes by other lightkeepers. In 1951, Eugene Gillan slipped and fell 40 metres from the top of the rock before bounding a further 55 metres to land in a soft pile of brush. I was present in 1973 when another keeper was saved from almost certain death by one of his colleagues, who broke his fall as he hurtled down towards a concrete pit. Tom Joyce was afterwards awarded a gold medal by the Commissioners for his courage.

The Tearaght is one of the Blasket Islands, a fact not commonly known. It lies between the Foze Rocks – the most westerly of our islands – and the mainland. In all probability, it was connected at one time to both the Foze and the mainland, but today it has the distinction of being one of the highest of these rocks, rising to 180 metres. Despite its height, the keepers maintained a spectacular garden on the only flat part of the island, just below the peak. One would have to be strong in wind and limb, and have the agility of a goat in order to undertake this highly dangerous trip. It led the climber along precarious paths that frequently disappear due to the natural rock falls, and the destructive undermining of the countless rabbits and goats. The near extinction of the latter has done much to alleviate the harm being done to the terrain. On arrival at the garden, however, the feeling was one of extreme satisfaction, having once again conquered the route. No thought was given to the return journey, which could be even more hazardous as it was a slippery downhill slide all the way. The garden itself produced enough fresh vegetables for the keepers' requirements for most of the year, but the burrowing rabbits that have been known to defy the 5 metres of heavy gauge netting-wire that surrounded the garden needed to be watched. All in all, the garden – hewn as it was out of an impoverished and unyielding soil – must surely lay claim to being the original 'God's Little Acre'. From the garden, it is not far to the summit, although this last part of the journey is practically straight up. But on reaching it, the spectacular view defies description. Up there, one is 'monarch of all I survey'. The other Blasket Islands and Carrantwohill are within hailing distance, and even the presence of a distinguished neighbour in Inishvickillaune pales into insignificance. At the very peak, a weathervane is set into the rock to aid navigation. In a natural crevice at its base, a thick diary was kept, wrapped in a weatherproof bag. Here, the thoughts and aspirations of all who made it to the summit were recorded. But it would appear from the many highly evocative entries I read that not all of them were enhanced by their sojourn on the Tearaght.

Before the lighthouse was built, there was much speculation as to whether or not the Foze Rocks was a more suitable place on which to construct it. After much deliberation and visits to both places, it was decided to site it on the highest rock. So the lighthouse was built on the Tearaght, and the light first exhibited in 1870. The tower itself is quite small, it being in such an elevated position, and there is a connecting corridor to the keepers' quarters. The engine room and fog signal are close by, and a helicopter pad has been created. The aerial hoist is still maintained for landing heavy materials, and the derricks are kept in working order. The light can be seen for 27 nautical miles, and has an intensity of 1.75 million candelas. ✱*Fl (2) W 20s*##

Little Samphire Island

Little Samphire Island was sanctioned as a lighthouse in 1848 following much inducement from the merchants and ship owners of Tralee. Plans were submitted, and it was agreed that ground should be purchased for the project. Adverse weather conditions prevented the commencement of work until 1849, and progress was so slow that it was not until 1852 that the tower was completed. It took a further two years before the light was exhibited. On 1 July 1854, the first light shone from Little Samphire. It was a fixed (non-flashing) light with red and white sectors. The tower, built of natural blueish limestone, is 13.5 metres high and the light is 17 metres above high water. The station was designed by Inspector Halpin and built by the Board's tradesmen. A single dwelling housed the principal keeper, and his wife acted as assistant keeper.

A local currach from Fenit attended the station two or three

Little Samphire Island

times a week. The light was converted to unwatched in 1954, and acetylene generators were installed. A further improvement in the light became necessary in 1976 when it was discovered that the increased background shore lighting was swamping the light. A decision was taken to convert to electricity, and a much improved light now shines from Little Samphire.

It has been a long time since I was at Samphire, but I remember the local attendant, Mr Crowley, and his wife very well, and the kindness and hospitality shown to me on all occasions. My first visit happened to coincide with the start of the Tralee Festival, and the weather was inclement enough to prevent a passage being made to the lighthouse. Funny thing is that it remained exactly like that for the ten days of the festival. I might add that I also had a good time at the races. Things were like that in those days! *Fl WRG 5s

Scattery Island

Scattery Island

As we make our way up the west coast, it is worth noting that, were it not for the magnificent River Shannon, there would have been no need for a lighthouse in this area at all. As it is, this sprawling estuary is very well served by Scattery Island, Tarbert, Kilcredaune and the Beeves Rock way out in the middle of the river. Dominating this scene is that sentinel-like lighthouse at Loop Head. I feel a special affinity with the Shannon area. Aside from its scenic beauty, I have found the people who dwell along its shores to be both intelligent and imaginative, and they avail of both the simple assets and the commercial opportunities that this great river affords.

Scattery Island lighthouse was one of the few 'movable' lights on our coast. These light structures were made of wood, and were deemed expendable when channel changes sometimes occurred. Where possible, the lighthouse would be dismantled and moved to a more suitable location. If necessary, a completely new tower would be built in its place. Scattery Island lighthouse is unique in that the reason for its being mobile was to keep it out of the firing line during army exercises. Whoever said lightkeeping was a nice, handy, safe job! ✳ *Fl (2) W 7.5s* ✳

Tarbert

Looking across the murky waters of the Shannon towards Tarbert in County Kerry, the twin ESB chimney stacks stand out like giants guarding the estuary. From Kilcredaune, Tarbert lighthouse is visible but not as clearly defined a light as it used to be, and it's clear that the whole scenario around this once beautiful island had changed dramatically. There was a time when Tarbert lighthouse dwarfed every other building for miles around, but now it is swamped by an advancing technological age. Its light is just another glow in the ESB galaxy, and one would wonder at the necessity of having a lighthouse there at all. But nautical tradition dies hard, and it will probably remain there for a long time to come. Incidentally, it is now under the control of the Limerick Harbour Board.

Tarbert was established in 1834 as a harbour light to guide vessels through Shannon estuary and to warn of the Bowline Rock; in1905, a red sector was established over the Bowline Rock. Built on a rock off the north side of Tarbert Island, the lighthouse is reached by means of a 200-foot-long, cast-iron foot bridge. The tower is painted white, and its light has a range of 13 nautical miles.

The ferry crossing from Kilimer takes no time at all, and is certainly a welcome innovation. The last time I was in Tarbert, I found the island I knew had disappeared. Even the buoy yard, once a dominant force, seemed strangely silent, and the abundance of green moss around the shore told its own sorry tale. I believe they don't even fish around this area any more.

The ESB has taken over in no uncertain manner. Both sides of the lighthouse compound are engulfed by the power-station complex, and massive storage tanks are everywhere. Incredibly ugly buildings, pylons and miles of cable have desecrated this once beautiful part of the estuary. It is certainly progress at a cost. The mile-long island road is a speed track, and no place for the casual visitor. The pub, which opened once a year on regatta day, is now a gold mine, and boasts no less than five pool tables.

There is no poverty in Tarbert now, but I remember when things were very different. On my first visit to Tarbert, the village was barely alive and jobs of any kind were at a premium. There was no need for our prefab near the lighthouse then, as every house in the village was more than keen to keep the few travellers that stopped over. I had digs for a pound a week, and even in those days that was dear. People were plentiful and jobs were scarce, and it was no problem getting men for the buoy yard. Locals vied with each other for the chance of a week's work. The big days were when a buoy had to be shipped to sea. For that major operation, up to ten men inched the old gantry towards the end of the pier, whence the steamer would take over. This was a slow and tedious procedure, and must have been irksome to the waiting tender. Then came the famous occasion when it was decided to hurry things up a bit. A line was tied to the crane from the steamer, and crane and buoy were got to the pier's end in record time. Unfortunately, the crane did not stop there, and came to rest with its front wheels dangling over the water's edge. A repair crew had to be sent from the depot to jack it up and return it to base. That operation was not tried again. But no such problems arise now, as a brand new gantry has been installed, and press-button switches do the rest. This is just as well, as labour is no longer available in Tarbert. The ESB has absorbed all the available manpower.

I lately walked towards the village, and noted with pleasure that the little wood is still there. Evermore, or 'Leslie's wood', still retains its dark, foreboding appearance. As I climbed over the rusted entrance gate and strolled along the overgrown paths where I once spent (or lost) some of my youth, I had almost a palpable feeling of a very special girl being right there beside me. I recalled the awful curse on the Leslie family that would deter any crow from nesting in their wood – a curse that seems to still hold sway, as the absence of bird life is very evident. The old abbey – where the monks were tortured and had their ears cut off by Cromwell's men – is still discernible, but the ravages of time have taken their toll. The story goes that when the abbey was sacked, the then land-lord, Leslie, did nothing to help the monks, and when one of the family was buried in the abbey afterwards, the birds left and never returned.

The battery that protected the estuary is gone. This had walls 2.25 metres thick, every stone weighing half a ton and leaded into position. I met a man who took part in a *feis* on top of this battery, and even won a prize for step-dancing. The row of little houses to the left of the secu-rity gate are all but gone, with only two still occupied.

There was much gaiety, laughter and loyalty among the island folk in those days, and even though it was an island in name only, they stuck to their heritage. I spent many a good night there, particularly in one house – alas, now a heap of rubble. The deafening overload of steam and the constant barrage of hooters have successfully taken over, and left a jungle of steel in their wake. The village itself, strangely enough, has not altered much structurally, but has a definite air of prosperity. Neon lights and garish counters are a feature of the bars, only one of which retains the same ownership. I went looking for a room in my old digs, but they had not had a vacancy in fifteen years. A whole ham and a dozen cooked chickens adorned the kitchen table, but I did not have the heart to remind the old lady of the times she had to borrow a half-crown from me to buy my own dinner. We did recall, though, the night I began and finished my 'fistic' career. It was regatta day, and a boxing ring was erected in the square. The local sergeant needed an opponent for a bit of exhibition sparring, and I foolishly accepted. Having imbibed well, but not too wisely, and looking forward to the dance that night, I felt good as I climbed into the ring. The first tap from the sergeant and I was out cold. I woke up in bed at about 8pm, and got up to get ready for the dance. Out on the street, everything seemed ominously quiet. It was some time before I realised it was the following day, and the fun was all over. I had been asleep for 24 hours.

It is still a lovely run back to Foynes, with some magnificent uninterrupted views across the Shannon. Looking back at Tarbert, one can only hope that no further desecration of this beautiful estuary is planned.

✱*Iso WR 4s*

Corlis Point

The romantic image of a lighthouse conjures up a tall, slender and curvaceous phalanx, dutifully fulfilling its lonely assignment to warn seafarers of the dangers awaiting those that stray. Such an idyll is rudely shattered when confronted with the leading lights of Corlis Point, established in 1998 to assist shipping to navigate the narrow waters between Kilcredaune Point and Kilconly Point. Though the rear light may feel it qualifies as Irish Light's least attractive specimen, I believe the front light at Corlis Point can rightfully claim the title. Because though the rear is nothing less than a light atop a pylon, the front light amounts to nothing more than several lanterns fixed to a hideous concrete box. Really, the less said about them the better. Except to acknowledge that both lights can legitimately claim to provide as good a service as any in the employ of Irish Lights, frills or no. ✳ *Front: Oc W 5s · Rear: Oc W 5s*

Kilcredaune

Kilcredaune, built in 1824, is a minor lighthouse on the northern peninsula of the estuary, at the end of a narrow, pot-holed boreen, a couple of miles from the village of Carrigaholt. Though quite a large tower, its peculiar location prevents it being actually sighted from land until one is right inside the light-house compound. Indeed, many of the students who spend their summers at the nearby Irish College are surprised when the teachers announce a trip to the lighthouse. It has been in the care of the same family for many years, and is currently attended by Jimmy

Kilcredaune

Rowan. He and his wife, together with an old man affectionately known as 'Cookie' Ryan, took excellent care of their charge. Cookie, now sadly deceased, was an excellent typist and a remarkable reader of Braille. He acquired his name having spent many years as a cook in the college at Ring. Speaking of the Rowans, I might add that Mrs Rowan herself makes the most delicious scones and delectable jams, and I usually climbed a few pounds on the scales after a visit there. *Fl W 6s*

Loop Head

Loop Head

During our journey, I have described some unusual structures from which lights were exhibited. Loop Head falls into this category, as the first known light on this headland was similar to those at the Baily and the Old Head of Kinsale. This stone-vaulted cottage had a naked light burning on a platform on the roof, and the small room adjacent to the fireplace was called 'Smith's shop'. This gives rise to the conjecture that the light-keeper served a dual role in the area. The light probably fell into disuse towards the end of the seventeenth century, because there is evidence of it being re-established in 1720 following complaints from the Limerick merchants. The remains of the old cottage can even now be identified, and the sturdy pillar on which the fire platform was built still survives.

Today, Loop Head, remotely located at the very tip of the Shannon estuary, is a very important lighthouse, and contains all the navigational aids requisite to our seagoing tradition. The cottage lighthouse, with its coal fire, was replaced in 1802 by a more conventional lighthouse. Built by Thomas Rogers, the tower was about the same height as the present one – 23 metres – with four rooms and a lantern approximately 84 metres above high water. The ground-floor room was an oil store, and access to the first floor, or entrance room, was by an outside staircase of nineteen steps. An internal spiral staircase connected the other two rooms and lantern. By 1811, the keeper was living in an adjoining cottage. The lantern – its diameter 3.5-metres – contained twelve oil lamps, each with its own concave parabolic reflector. The reflected light shone through a 7-metre-diameter convex lens of solid glass, not unlike the 'bottle glass' or 'bullseye' fitted windows of modern, pseudo-Georgian houses. The number of oil lamps and reflectors in the lantern had been increased to fifteen by 1825.

During 1836, the Limerick Chamber of Commerce complained of the poor light, and went as far as suggesting that the tower be rebuilt. Having investigated the complaint, the inspector reported to the Board that the light was as good as most lights around the coast, and did not warrant immediate action. But seven years later – towards the end of 1843 – he did propose a new tower and optic. The Ballast Board agreed, and by June 1844, the seal was set on the contract for Mr William Burgess of Limerick to build a new tower, approximately 10 metres from the 1802 tower in an east-north-east direction. The new tower, designed by George Halpin, was completed early in 1854, and took over from the 1802 tower on 1 May. As the two towers were almost identical in height, the lantern of the old tower had to be completely removed during daylight hours prior to the night of 1 May, so as not to obstruct the new light when it came into operation. The optic was a first-order dioptric lens with an oil lamp in its focus, giving a fixed, or non-flashing, light. In September 1866, sanction was given to alter the light from fixed to intermittent. This was achieved by rotating a screen around the lamp to give a character of 20 seconds light followed by 4 seconds dark. The screen was rotated by a weight-driven clockwork machine. The new intermittent light came into operation in March 1869.

An explosive signal was established in 1898, giving one report every 10 minutes. This was changed in 1919 to one every 5 minutes, and again in 1934, to one in every 4 minutes. The explosive fog signal was discontinued in 1972. The light was improved in 1912, and its character altered to four flashes every 20 seconds. Conversion to electricity occurred in 1971, and the optic is now driven by an electric motor, rather than the clockwork rotation machine. ✳ *Fl (4) W 20s*

Blackhead, Clare

Blackhead, Clare

Galway Bay, from early in the nineteenth century, had been recognised as a good harbour and shelter, the Aran Islands giving it a natural barrier from the southwesterlies. Fishing was one of the main forms of employment in this area, the land around Galway being mainly of rocky or stony character, and not conducive to extensive farming as practised in the more fertile parts of the country. The first lighthouse to be established in Galway Bay – in 1817 – was on Mutton Island, off Salthill; in effect, a harbour light for Galway. On Inishmore, the largest of the Aran Islands, a light was established in 1818.

While not decrying Blackhead in any way, and agreeing that it serves an important function on the Galway–Clare coast, it is only fair to say that its relative importance is greatly overshadowed by such lights as Loop Head, Hook Tower and the Baily. But like its counterpart in Charlesfort, it is immaculately maintained and I believe it is true of this particular lighthouse that the attendant takes such pride in its appearance that, on the morning of the annual inspection, he rakes the gravel path one final time, taking care to travel backwards so as to ensure that no footprint will spoil its appearance. Such dedication to detail! Yet the dedicated maintenance of our lighthouses is no more than a continuation of the time, effort and patience it takes to establish even the most insignificant of our lighthouses. The establishment of the Blackhead light illustrates this process as well as any.

Blackhead is located in An Bhoireann – the Burren, or the stony district – which forms the northern part of County Clare, bounded by the south shore of Galway Bay to the north, the Atlantic Ocean to the west, Gortaclare mountains to the east, with Lisdoonvarna, Kilfenora and Corrofin to the south – well over 250 square kilometres of unique limestone. In *Ludlow's Memoirs* (1651), penned by a general in charge of the Cromwellian forces in County Clare, this poetic description of the Burren is offered: 'Not a tree whereon to hang a man, no water in which to drown him, no soil in which to bury him.'

Notwithstanding the Depression of the 1930s, transatlantic liners called regularly at Galway, either delivering tourists to visit the city and the Aran Islands, or collecting emigrants. Cunard had a monthly westbound scheduled call, and the SS *Dún Aengus*, of 1912 vintage, acted as a tender to the Cunarders, and to any other liners that called. The captains of these visiting liners were instrumental in ensuring a lighthouse was built on Blackhead. They used to anchor their vessels off Ballyvaghan, east of Blackhead. A letter from the Galway Harbour Commissioners referred to the Galway harbour master's report of continuous complaints from captains of liners using Galway port. They stated that a light on Blackhead would be of great assistance to all vessels anchoring under the headland. Captain Davies, an inspector and marine superintendent, and Mr Tonkin, chief engineer, discussed the request with the Galway Commissioners, and asked whether a lighthouse on Blackhead was more important than a wireless beacon on Eeragh. Though the Galway Commissioners had to agree that the latter was more important, it never materialised. Erecting a light on a repayment basis was also discussed. Consideration for this was given by the Galway Commissioners, and in their reply of 11 October 1934 they stated that a wireless beacon on North Aran was of importance, but a light on Blackhead was an imminent and urgent necessity. They also stated that they would consider repayment of costs to Irish Lights over a short period. Towards the end of October, Mr Tonkin estimated that the capital cost would be £1,730, and the annual cost of maintenance would be £45, in addition to the attendant's salary.

In November 1834, the Galway Commissioners agreed to Irish Lights erecting the light. The concrete tower was built by Mr Robert MacDonald of Galway. Chance Brothers of Birmingham supplied the fourth-order optic. Steven and Struthers of Glasgow provided the lantern. Glass for the lantern was by Seddon and Sons of St Helen's, Lancashire. W. Moyes of Glasgow supplied the twin 25.4 kilogram generators for the carbide-to-water acetylene generating plant. They also supplied the flashers. The tower measures 4 metres square by 5.1 metres high.

During July 1934, the Galway Commissioners requested that a red sector be provided to cover Loo Rock, and that the Finnis Rock buoy off Inisheer be lit. The Board agreed to provide a red sector for Blackhead, but referred the lighting of the Finnis buoy to the Inspecting Committee. The latter was not lit until 1978. Towards the end of August 1934, Mr Tonkin interviewed Mr John Casey, the prospective attendant, who lived with his family near the lighthouse at Morrough. If the Galway Commissioners agreed to his employment, he would be offered £12 per annum, plus a further £2 for painting the tower at least once a year. The appointment was from the exhibition of the light.

Due to unforeseen circumstances, faults in the construction of the lantern by Stevens and Struthers caused delay in its completion, and it was not dispatched from Glasgow until early December 1935. When the tower was complete, the acetylene gear was to be transported to the tower. A delay was caused by an error on the part of the lantern glass supplier, and when templates were held up by British customs when being returned to Seddon and Sons. Yet further delay was caused when Irish customs held up the new glass – ironically, it was too big, and a Dublin firm had to be engaged to grind the edges. Meanwhile, temporary glazing was fitted into the lantern, and the light was established on 21 February 1936. The correct glass was fitted a few days later, and the light was checked on 29 April 1936 by Captain Holinshead, commander of the Irish Lights tender, *Isolda*.

With the outbreak of the Second World War in 1939, transatlantic liners ceased to call at Galway. In post-war years, traffic failed to revive, and coastal traffic was similarly affected. As the Galway Harbour Commissioners did not collect light dues for Blackhead, it became an increasing financial burden on their resources, especially when the attendant looked for a further £2 per week! Much bureaucratic procrastination eventually led to an agreement whereby Irish Lights would take over Blackhead lighthouse from the Galway Harbour Commissioners. In April 1955, Captain W.H. Ball, assistant inspector, and Mr A.D.H.

Martin, deputy chief engineer, proceeded to Blackhead and found the tower in an excellent state of repair and tidy condition. Captain Ball interviewed John Casey, whom he recommended be retained as attendant keeper. He would receive the appropriate remuneration for the class of station into which Blackhead fell, which for Mr Casey meant an immediate increase of £30 on his previous salary. Mr Martin, realising that Mr Casey had to cycle 4.8 kilometres twice a day to turn on the light – 1 hour before sunset – and to extinguish it – an hour after sunrise – recommended a Newbridge 15-day-clock gas valve be fitted. Mr Casey thought it was his birthday – what with the extra money and without the prospect of having to cycle 6 miles a day, every day, as he had done for the previous nineteen years. Captain Ball collected the deeds, and the property was formally accepted.

In September 1977, it was proposed to convert the light to propane, as the carbide-to-water acetylene generators were old and obsolete. Blackhead was the last of many stations around the coast to use carbide-to-water acetylene generators. The conversion was to be included in the 1980–81 estimates, and Department of Trade sanction was obtained in March 1980. The existing character of a 0.4-second flash every 2 seconds was unsuitable, so a 1-second flash every 5 seconds was agreed between the inspector and the engineer. The Board approved the change on 13 June 1980, and the Notice to Mariners was issued on 18 September 1980.

On 12 November 1980, Mr John Casey informed the Commissioners that he intended to retire at the end of the month, and recommended that his son, Joseph, take his place. John was persuaded to 'hang on' for another month for administrative purposes. He was 68 years old, had been attendant for nearly 26 years with Irish Lights and, prior to that, had spent nineteen years with the Galway Harbour Commissioners. Joseph Casey took over from his father on 1 January 1981. *Fl WR 5s*

In the early 1850s, it was decided that the tower in operation on Inishmore – at an altitude of 122 metres – was so ineffective in cloudy or misty weather that two new towers should be erected, one on Eeragh (also known as North Aran or Rock Island), at the north-west end of the Arans, and the other on Inisheer, at the south-east end. The two towers, built simultaneously, were sited almost at sea level. Chance Brothers of Birmingham supplied the fixed optic for Inisheer, and Wilkins of London the flashing optic for Eeragh. The towers and keepers' dwellings were built of the local, very hard, crystalline limestone, and each consequently sport distinguished coloured bands. The lights were first exhibited on 1 December 1857, after a delay of a month due to bad weather. Both lights are now automated, and in the care of local attendants.

If I had a preference for one of the Aran Islands, I think it must be

Inisheer

Inishmaan, but since we do not maintain a lighthouse there, I shall have to settle for Inisheer. This island, still unspoilt, holds many happy memories for me, and I recall fondly the parties that the visiting *Gaeltacht* children used to hold in the lighthouse. This happy, carefree bunch added a new dimension to the station during the summer. Mind you, I never heard any of them speaking Irish, at least not out of earshot of the teachers. What a pity those parties are no more, and what a pity also that lights such as Inisheer should have become automated, especially since it was such a favourite station with keepers and maintenance staff alike.

✹ Iso WR 12s

Eeragh

The story of Eeragh's lighthouse is virtually identical to its twin on Inisheer, and so the reader can refer to that entry for its history. When heading for either lighthouse, shopping would first be undertaken in Galway city, before embarking for Inisheer or Eeragh by steamer. Getting to the former was easy enough, but getting to Eeragh – or North Aran, as it is sometimes called – was problematical. The arrival on Inishmore was only the beginning of the journey; then came the hard part. Lodgings could usually be found in Kilronan, where the steamers anchored, but the departure point for the rock was way back in Bungowla, about 6 miles away. Eeragh was one of the hardest places on which to land. Though only a short distance from the main island, the passage was invariably rough and daunting, and the frail but sturdy currach is the only craft suitable for landing on the sandy beaches around the islands.

On my first visit to Aran, I made the journey on a side cart from Kilronan to Bungowla on eight consecutive mornings, hoping against hope to get to the rock. The weather was bitterly cold, and every morning, I had to hang around for hours, without any shelter, waiting for the boatmen to make up their minds whether or not they were going to attempt the journey. All the time, I was conscious of the basket of decaying grub purchased in Galway a week earlier – it could not be stored in a fridge as such contraptions had yet to reach the island. Eventually, one morning, the activity commenced. Scurrying feet protruding from under the currach carried the boat in record time down to the sea. As is the custom, I climbed on the back of one of the crew, who waded out with me and unceremoniously dumped me into the boat. Baskets, boxes and bales followed. Somehow, the oars worked, and we were on our way to Eeragh. After all the inactivity of the previous days, the action on relief day was decidedly perplexing. Instructions about behaviour and procedure were all in Irish, and the continuous babble of voices, together with a constant waving of arms in all directions, made me not one whit wiser as to the goings-on. But one instruction was clearly and forcefully communicated to me as I attempted to stand up in the currach so as to get a better view of my surroundings; a mighty hand grabbed me from behind and nearly dislocated a shoulder. I quickly decided the scenery was not that important.

I did not find Eeragh the most interesting of stations. Although covering a large area, it was a flat, barren rock, and devoid of character. But it was on this lighthouse that I met one of those characters who made our often tedious life on the coast quite bearable. This fellow's name was Bill, and he was one of our coastal painters. In those days, our painters had probably one of the most unenviable jobs of all the maintenance staff employed on the coast. Among their number was Brendan Behan, who once quipped, 'Myself and Winston Churchill were once upon a time in the same organisation: he as an Elder Brother of Trinity House and I as a painter for the Irish Lights. His position is more decorative than functional. I painted striped lighthouses, banded lighthouses and spotted

Eeragh

lighthouses.' Travelling from lighthouse to lighthouse, without a base of any kind and very little home leave (official anyway), their lot was not a coveted one. The compensatory part of it was that they could – and did – spend quite inordinately long periods of time at every station in which they worked. I can recall two of them at Valentia, painting eight houses for fourteen months. But time was not a factor in those days – not alone for the painters, but for any of us. Indeed, Irish Lights seemed to appreciate the fact that they had, in their employment, people who were willing to spend very long periods away from home working in the most isolated and inaccessible places. But back to Bill. I believe he gave me more laughs than anyone I ever met on the coast. We came ashore from North Aran together, and had to leave by the same piggyback method. I managed to get into the currach in a fairly dry condition, but poor Bill was a lot heavier than his fellow with the rubber boots, and the two of them fell into the tide. The language, naturally, was choice, but suffice to say that when we both eventually reached Galway, after a dreadful passage by trawler to Rosaveal, I deemed it prudent to make my own way home. No such luck, though. We both had to stay the night in Galway, and the American Hotel was then our watering hole in that part of the country. I decided on a low profile that evening, but passing by the lounge, I spied the bold Bill sitting on a high stool, clad only in a dressing gown. He had borrowed it from the manager while his own clothes were drying out in the boiler room. Although 'well on' at this stage, he spotted me, and we were the focus of some rapt attention for the rest of the evening.

On another occasion, I brought Bill to look at what was then the new cathedral, and suggested we both go to confession. Having not been for twenty years, he thought it was a good idea. Almost immediately, a startled crowd outside the box – myself included – were subjected to a fierce argument between himself and the priest, and next thing, Bill came out and exclaimed to all and sundry: 'Imagine asking if I ever took pleasure in bad thoughts! What the bloody hell does he think they're for, anyway?' That ended Bill's relationship with the confessional. I don't know where you are now, Bill, but good luck to you, wherever it is. You certainly brightened up many a dull and miserable day on the coast.

✳ Fl W 15s

Straw Island

Our next and last port of call on Aran is Straw Island. Most people on the boat from Galway to Aran cannot help but notice this rather small light on the way to Kilronan. Uninhabited now, it was home for many of the keepers and their families since 1878. A light had been sought by the locals on this island since 1854 – remember, there were over 3,000 vessels from Claddagh fishing the area then – and foreseeing the imminent closure of the light on Inishmore, sanction was given for the lighthouse in 1871. The newly constructed tower was painted white and equipped with a fixed red light. The light was made group flashing white in 1926, and was another of the carbide-to-water kind. A major change took place on 23 August 1980 when the light was made electric. Batteries supplied the power for the optic, necessitating the erection of a wind generator to charge the batteries. The use of wind generators is becoming increasingly popular on the coast, and those already in use are extremely efficient.

A word here about the durable materials used, even for a small lighthouse such as that at Straw Island. A few years ago, when the local fishermen complained that the island was becoming so silted up with sand that the light was obscured at various points, it was decided to raise the height of the light. As the top pier of glass in the lantern was blanked off, it was necessary to renew this when relocating the light. Only then was it discovered that the blank 'panes' were in fact copper plates 50 millimetres square by 12 millimetres thick. These must have been fairly expensive even in those days, and were afterwards used as lightning-conductor anchor plates for various towers around the coast.

It was on Straw Island that I learnt something of the peculiar system that nature has of protecting its own. Rats and seagulls were plentiful on the island, but there was no danger of overcrowding by either species, as the rats varied their diet by eating the gulls' eggs, and the gulls killed many of the rats. Quite a nice little cancellation exercise, this. Here, I ate my first gulls' eggs, and learnt never to take any from the nest when there were three in it as three is the maximum number of eggs a gull lays and these might have been there for some time; nests holding one or two eggs were fairly sure to have fresh ones.

I seem to have spent a lot of my time on Straw Island, or to be more precise, in trying to get to it, as it was not the most accessible of islands. In Kilronan, though, I had very pleasant digs at St Kevin's guest house, run by a Mr and Mrs Joyce. When not at the lighthouse, I used to assist in the restaurant, serving meals to the day trippers from Galway. As many of the visitors were sick after the journey, a lot of tact was needed when bills were presented – the meals would have been ordered by phone the previous day, and so had to be paid for. ✳ *Fl (2) W 5s*

Straw Island

Cashla Bay

Some lights perform their task without fanfare, and Cashla Bay must surely fall into this category. Admittedly, it's still in its infancy when compared to some of our centuries-old sentinels – Cashla Bay directional light came into being in 1984 – and it's not much to look at: a white, square, concrete tower atop a column. Nor is it very high: a mere 4 metres. But it does its job to the best of its ability, and those trawlermen seeking the entrance at night into Cashla Bay appreciate its assistance in ensuring safe passage no less than the captains of majestic liners once appreciated the blink emanating from the Fastnet.

Though the lighthouse has gone unsung, Cashla Bay itself has achieved a kind of recognition in literature. The late-nineteenth-century writer and poet, Emily Lawless, in her 1892 novel, *Grania*, describes the area, though in uncomplimentary terms:

> The road from Cashla Bay past Spiddal into Galway is as grim a
> one surely as is to be found in these three kingdoms. Mile after
> mile it runs through a grey world of boulders, varying from the
> size of a hencoop to that of an average cottage.

I rather like the sound of a place like that – it's a pity there are so few of them these days. By the way, Cashla is a derivative of the Irish *caisle*, meaning a small inlet. ✳ *Dir Iso WRG 4s*

Slyne Head

Continuing on our way up the west coast, we come to another of those places that require skill, tact and not a little patience before our destination is finally reached. I think it can be safely said that no more intriguing journey – in these islands, anyway – had to be undertaken before one landed on Slyne Head, a place known only to most people through its association with the daily weather forecast. Younger keepers no doubt scoffed at the idea of donkeys being used to carry out a relief, especially in modern times, but this can be verified by many of the not-so-old hands in the service. Indeed, a recently retired engineer-in-chief, Mr A.D.H. Martin, wrote a very descriptive account of such a trip to Slyne Head in our service magazine, *Beam*. This particular relief was for a long time known as 'The Long Journey into Egypt'. Clifden was the main 'town' en route to our destination, and having found a place to stay, it was necessary to report to the keeper ashore to let him know there would be an extra passenger on the boat for the relief. This procedure was always done on the night of one's arrival, though the relief might not be carried out for days, sometimes even weeks. When the big day arrived, Packie King – the long-time boatman – having decided that everything was right for the journey, would hoist a bat at a stone wall near his cottage to let the keepers on the rock know that the relief was imminent. Next, he would proceed to Bunowen to inform the car contractor, Packie Sweeney. More often than not, this journey had to be made by horseback, as the bicycle was usually out of commission. When ready, we all set off from Clifden for what was known as the 'End of the Road' – aptly named, as it was literally the end of the road. It terminated at a place known locally as the 'Curfield', where before the war an enterprising aviation entrepreneur, Sir Alan Cobham, held his flying circus. Once the road finished, a

Slyne Head

horse took over. After that, it was donkeys for the remainder of the journey through gorse, rocks and heather for about a mile until we reached Slackport, from where the currach would be rowed out the 3 miles through islands and rocks to Slyne Head. What a beautiful experience that was, especially when the weather relented, and it could be fully enjoyed.

Ceann Léim, or Leap Head, is formed by a chain of rocks and islands off the mainland, 16 kilometres southwest of Clifden, and not far from where those intrepid British aviators, Captain J.W. Alcock and Lieutenant A. Whitten-Brown, crash-landed their Vickers Vimy in a bog near the Marconi wireless station on the morning of 15 June 1919, almost 16 hours after taking off from St John's, Newfoundland. The name Slyne is an anglicised corruption of *léim* – meaning 'leap'. Leap also forms part of the name given to the island closest to the mainland in the Slyne Head archipelago: Illaunaleama, or Leap Island. The actual island upon which the lighthouse station is positioned is called Illaunamid on the 6-inch Ordnance Survey map, and Illaunimmul on the Admiralty chart. It is the largest and most westerly of the islands forming Slyne Head, and is composed of a rock called gneiss.

An unsuccessful request for a light on Slyne Head was made in 1819 by Captain C.S. Whyte of HMS *Cyprus*, a vessel that belonged to the coastguard then stationed between Broadhaven and Loop Head. It was not until the end of 1830 that things began to move for Slyne Head. Numerous memorials from the coastguard, the mayor, merchants and ship owners of Galway – together with those of the inhabitants of Roundstone and Clifden – sought improvements to the lighting on the west coast. Lighthouses at Slyne Head, Blackrock (north of Achill Island) and Eagle Island were mentioned. In his report, Inspector George Halpin recommended two lighthouses with revolving lights at Slyne Head, so as not to be confused with Clare Island to the north and Inishmore to the south. He also recommended two stationary lights at Eagle Island; here, again, so as to avoid confusion, this time with Clare Island to its south and Aranmore to the north. Inspector Halpin designed and supervised the construction of the towers, dwellings (two per station) and outhouses, all of which were built by the Board's tradesmen. Stone from the island seems to have been used for much of the buildings and walls, though granite and sandstone were also brought onto the island. A coppersmith named John Smith covered the two domes towards the end of 1835 for £60 each, and in March 1836, J. Dove of Edinburgh was engaged to construct the revolving machinery for one of the lighthouses; only one of the lights was to be revolving, though sanction in 1830 had been for both lights.

During the building of the stations, two boating accidents occurred. The first was in early 1832 when a man named Hallam lost his life while carrying stones. Afterwards, his wife and four children were awarded twenty guineas. The other was on 27 March 1836 when a boat overturned and eight men were drowned. Pensions of £6 per annum were awarded to two widows, one of whom lost her husband and a son; £3 per annum was paid for children under sixteen years of age; and a donation of £3 was made to each of three sisters who were supported by one of the men.

By June 1836, Inspector Halpin reported that the lighthouses would be ready for lighting on 10 October, though there was still a lot more work required to complete the stations. The towers were painted white and were virtually identical – a few minor differences were to be found in floor height and internal granite stairs. The 1875 Admiralty list of lights states that the towers were 24 metres from base to vane, and 130 metres apart. The south tower, although discontinued since 1898, still retains much of its slate weather-hanging, but strong winds are slowly peeling off the slates. The cost of the two stations to the end of the year 1840 was a little over £40,000 – a lot of money in those days when compared to mainland stations such as Ferris Point and Broadhaven, which cost around £7,000 each.

Another boating accident occurred in Slyne Head's early years – on 22 October 1852. At that time, keepers and their families lived at stations on both the mainland and on rocks. A keeper had gone ashore to make arrangements to convey his wife and five children to Kilcredaune, and was drowned along with the boat crew of six while returning to the rock. The keepers on the rock had seen the boat coming, but it never arrived on the landing. Neither the boat nor the bodies were ever recovered. A revered silence is still maintained when passing this place, known locally as 'Floggers Point'. It is poignant to note that of the six boatmen, three were named King – a father and his two sons, I believe. The King family at Slyne Head held the boat contract for a very long time. Packie King's father, John King, who died in 1921, had been the contractor for many years before that, and was succeeded by his widow, Mrs Annie King, who handed it over to her son in 1946. The

Slyne Head

contract, which had been in the King family since 1850, was held up until the helicopter took over in 1969. Packie King, the last of the King family to act as boat contractor to Slyne Head, died on 11 April 1977, thus ending one of the longest tenures of boatmen in the service.

The two lights on Slyne Head were exhibited until 1898 when it was decided to discontinue one of the towers and improve the remaining light. The fog-signal apparatus on Slyne Head was quite different from those at other stations, where the explosive charge was attached to one end of a jib, and swung up and detonated above the lantern, or firing-house roof. At Slyne, a special rail was attached to the lantern balcony, outside the railing, on which ran a rope-operated circular carriage. One of the windows of the upper floor was converted to a door – with a porch – so the keeper could attach the explosive charges to a bracket hanging down from the carriage, then use the rope to turn the carriage through 160° to the opposite side of the tower, where a baffle had been set up close to the window to 'reflect' the explosion, and to prevent damage to the tower and lantern. This unusual type of explosive fog signal lasted until 1951, except for a period between 1941 and 1948. In 1951, a new fog-signal house was built in the north-west corner of the compound, and the charges were attached to the end of a jib. All explosive fog signals around the coast were discontinued in 1974.

During the Second World War, three local incidents were reported by the keepers. On two occasions, shipwrecked mariners came onto the island and went to the mainland using the contractor's boat. The third incident involved an American Liberator aircraft, which crashed near Lough Aillebrack on the mainland, 6 kilometres northeast of the lighthouse. The crew of the Liberator were not as lucky as Alcock and Browne 25 years earlier; one was killed and the others were taken to hospital in Clifden. ✳ *Fl (2) W 15s*

Inishgort

Clew Bay has an island for every day of the year. Mind you, many of them are no bigger than a large clump of rocks, but hardly anyone is likely to take the trouble to refute that suspiciously precise number. On the outside limits of this beautiful bay, and not too far from the Atlantic proper, lies the island of Inishgort, on which can be found a small, whitewashed lighthouse. Built from limestone in 1828, its light has a range of 10 nautical miles, and must surely be one of the loneliest of its kind on any of the islands. Yet the one family has lived, farmed and tended this lonely outpost for many years.

On Inishgort, I met some of those unique people who make up the backbone of many of our island families. When I first went to stay in Inishgort, there were two brothers living in the lighthouse – Bill and Tommy Jeffers. Though Bill was the appointed attendant, the only obvious difference between the two brothers was that Bill wore a service cap. We were all living in the same house, and it was not long before I noticed something rather odd: they never spoke to each other. Instinct borne of routine seemed to determine their every move. From long experience in isolation, each was fully aware of what the other was doing at any given moment. When there was a need to communicate through spoken language, each of the brothers addressed the other through a third person. Though they never spoke to each other, neither could they live without one another – the boat, a piece of barren land and the few cattle they kept required their combined attention.

We had a provision boat every Friday, and the three of us would go to Westport in this fragile craft, powered by an outboard motor. More often than not, we had to row, sometimes both ways, as the engine was not the most reliable. Bill was an asthmatic, and both drank plenty. How we managed to get back home many a night from town, God only

Inishgort

knows. Trying to steer the boat through all those islands in the daytime was daunting enough, even with the whole of one's senses.

Sometimes, when Bill had one of his attacks, the house would reek for days from the incense he used to gain relief from his suffering. The inhaling would go on for interminable hours, and sleep was impossible for anyone for days. Inevitably, Bill lost his long-drawn-out battle with his inhaler, and died a relatively young man. Tom was given the job of attendant, but it was not long before he became something of a recluse. Though the only other family on the island was another brother of Tom's, communication between them was nil.

I spent a lot of time with Tommy in his latter years, and we livened up Westport on many a Friday night. On the way home, we invariably called to Tommy Gibbons, a relative of Tom's on the island of Inishlyre, and there the bottle of whiskey and the half-dozen bottles of stout would be produced. The *craic* often went on all night, and it would be daylight before Tommy and I got home. The Gibbons were truly genuine people, and the most hospitable I have ever met. I well remember one occasion passing by their island on my way back to Dublin and being hailed to come to the pier, where I was presented with 4 pounds of homemade butter and a pair of live chickens, the latter being the source of much amusement to my fellow passengers on the train home.

I think Tommy Jeffers was the poorest man I ever met. He would wait for his paltry cheque from the middle of every month, yet he would never land on Inishlyre without bringing the usual liquid refreshments for his friends. I tried to advise him many times, but it was too late for Tommy. He was, towards the end, a fatalist, and life did not really amount to much for him. His death came about rather oddly, but in the circumstances, somewhat appropriately. He left a stonemason ashore to Westport, who had been working on the lighthouse, and apparently both had plenty of drink taken. Tommy went back out to his lighthouse, but the next morning was found dead in the boat. Strangely, it had drifted right onto the beach from where he and his brother Bill had launched it, in silence, many, many times in the past. ✳*Lfl W 10s*

Achillbeg

Achillbeg

On the way to our next port of call, we pass Achillbeg. I will not dwell long here, as it is an unpretentious little light, and not long in existence. It was built as an alternative to Clare Island when it was discovered that the lighthouse there was a lot less effective than had been hoped.

Unpretentious or not, Achillbeg does provide me with an anecdote. When I eventually decided that my bachelor days were over, and the matter of a honeymoon arose, the only suitable place in Ireland I could think of that did not have a lighthouse close by was Achill Island, so it was there that my wife and I spent the greater part of that happy occasion. Shortly after, it was decided that Achill was to be the base of the re-sited lighthouse, so it would appear we made it just in time.

The light was established on Achillbeg in 1965 as a replacement for nearby Clare Island whose light had been frequently obscured by low cloud and fog. Built in 1806, the suitability of the light on Clare Island was questioned as long ago as 1863. Yet the light was refurbished in 1909, and was scheduled for automation in 1958. Finally though, the game was up for Clare Island, and a sensible decision was taken to replace it with a light on Achillbeg. *Fl WR 5s*

Blacksod

I was sitting in a freezing bus from Ballina on a bleak October night, heading into the unknown. I had never heard of Blacksod. Even the very nature of my trip to Blacksod was strange. The bus conductor spent the entire journey relating his obviously thwarted love life to me, and as I would be staying in the same house as the lady in question, the consequences of any advances on my part were being fully communicated by this love-sick conductor. He need not have worried. While I have never been one to look a gift horse in the mouth, sitting there in that freezing bus, starving with the hunger, in the middle of nowhere, even the presence in Blacksod of my illustrious namesake, Elizabeth Taylor (Taylor, not Elizabeth), would have failed to raise a quiver in me.

If ever a place was aptly named, it was Blacksod. Located at what is very definitely the end of the road – the next parish is America – it is picturesquely situated on the south-west corner of the Mullet peninsula, backed by low-lying hills, with the magnificent backdrop of Achill Island to the south. Close to Blacksod are quarries of high-quality red granite, which over the years has been shipped to many parts of the world. A narrow-gauge tramway was laid from these quarries over the shoulder of the hill, down to the harbour and through the compound of dwellings for the lightkeepers attached to Blacksod lighthouse, 20 kilometres west of Blacksod. The tramway was operated partly by gravity and partly by a winch positioned on the shoulder of the hill that hauled the loaded wagons up the incline from the quarry, and the empty wagons back up the hill from the Blacksod shore-dwellings compound. The line was laid in 1889, taken up in 1900, re-laid in 1906, and taken up again in 1910, when it was relocated to Pickle Point on Broadhaven, 2.5 kilometres east of Belmullet. Whether it was even used here I have not been able to ascertain, but a pier at this point served Belmullet, and was used for over 40 years from the turn of the century by the Sligo Steam Navigation Company's vessel, SS *Tartar*. This vessel – subsidised by the government on behalf of the Congested Districts' Board – made regular runs to and from Sligo, calling at Rosses Point at the entrance to Sligo Harbour, and at Ballina, Ballycastle and Balderg on the north coast of County Mayo.

The need for a lighthouse at the southern extremity of the Mullet peninsula was first mentioned in 1841 in a letter from Lieutenant Nugent of the coastguard stationed at Belmullet. Had a navigational aid been in place 373 years earlier, it would have been of use to Mairtín de Berthendone – of the ill-fated *La Sancta Maria Rata Encoronda* of Philip II's armada – when de Berthendone turned into Blacksod Bay only to run aground near Doona (or Fahy Castle, as it is called today). The 1841 letter from Lieutenant Nugent requested that a lighthouse be placed on Blackrock, but Inspector George Halpin's report to the Board recommended against a light on Blackrock as a general sea light, and stated that a light on Blacksod Point – the Mullet's southern extremity – would be a useful light to lead vessels into Blacksod Bay. The subject was postponed until 1857, when it was again mentioned by the Inspecting Committee. Blackrock was sanctioned, but Blacksod Point had to wait a further four years.

In June 1861, the Inspecting Committee recommended placing a light on Blacksod Point, which, in conjunction with Blackrock, would make the latter a safe anchorage. Plans were submitted in September 1863 by Mr J.S. Sloan – the Board's superintendent of works – and were sent to Mr C.P. Cotton, the Board's consulting engineer, who approved the design. The Board of Trade's approval was obtained in October, subject to a slight modification: it suggested an octagonal lantern instead of a square one. The altered plans retained the two masonry sides of the square lantern, and introduced a semi-circular eight-sided glazed lantern seaward over the bay. In November, the secretary, Mr Lees, was instructed by the Board to apply to the proper quarter to obtain land. By December, the Reverend W. Palmer's offer to grant one statute acre of land for £1 per annum for lighthouse premises was approved. During May the following year – 1864 – the reverend gentleman, who also owned and worked the local granite quarries, wrote to the Board to offer granite for building at a sum of £100, to be paid for at the commencement of works. The light was first exhibited on 30 June 1866, and showed a fixed light with a red sector over Ardelly Point. In July 1877, sanction was granted by Trinity House and the Board of Trade for 'colouring' the tower white, with either paint or whitewash. Today, only the lantern is white. When the tower reverted to its reddish-grey colour, I have not been able to ascertain, but I have a suspicion that perhaps it was never painted or whitewashed; even the Victorians would have had respect for the very fine, reddish-grey, granite stonework.

At first, the relief keeper ashore from Blackrock looked after the light, but on 1 November 1933, Mr Edward Sweeney was appointed as attendant, and had the honour of being the second-longest-serving attendant on the coast. For the record, the longest-serving attendant – by eleven months – was Mr P. Byrne, at St John's Point, Donegal, while Mr J.J. Rowan, at Kilcredaune, took third place on 1 December 1938.

I saw my first (and only) domestic weather station in Blacksod. By an ingenious method of strategically placed pots, jam jars, weathervanes and an intuition gleaned from years of experience, Ted Sweeney ran his meteorological service for years from his back garden. It was a round-the-clock service as well, and necessitated the assistance of two local girls. I need hardly add that these were an added attraction to my duties at the lighthouse, though on one occasion I was barred by Ted's mother from the dwelling house. It was mid-afternoon, and in the act of chasing one of the girls around the kitchen, my coat got caught in the dresser. Cups, saucers and plates – some hundreds of years old – came crashing down. Ma Sweeney, brandishing a huge stick, hunted me out of the house and told me never to return. The old lady had already buried two husbands, and looked like dispatching me in the same direction. Nevertheless, back I was very shortly, as Ted was much too busy with the lighthouse, the weather station, the newly acquired post office and being involved in almost everything else that moved around Blacksod. Indeed, at times, in the absence of any females, I believe I helped rear not a few of Ted's children, and saw them grow to maturity over the years. The Sweeney name has a long association with Irish Lights, and Ted had three sons actively involved with the service. One succeeded him as attendant at Blacksod, another is an engineer aboard our service steamer, *Granuaile*, and the third is yet another lightkeeper, now attendant at Inishtrahull in Donegal.

I spent a lot of time in Blacksod, but like Castletownbere, it was usually an enforced stay on my way to Blackrock. Towards the end of 1969, however, Blacksod became the helicopter base for Eagle Island and Blackrock, and now boasts an 11-metre-diameter concrete helipad, store and waiting room. Gone are the days of having to wait patiently for the weather or the sea to improve before the relief boat could set out for Blacksod, and correspondingly, having to wait even more patiently to get ashore to replenish the food store. ✴ *Fl (2) WR 7.5s*

Blackrock, Mayo

In October 1830, the coastguard approached the Corporation for Improving the Port of Dublin (the forerunner of Irish Lights) to request lights for Slyne Head and Blackrock, north of Achill Island. The subject was referred to Inspector George Halpin; in his report, he agreed that Slyne Head warranted marking, but suggested Eagle Island in preference to Blackrock. The corporation was again approached by the coastguard in 1841, but Inspector Halpin still maintained that Eagle Island was better situated as a sea light, though he agreed that Blackrock would be a good guide for vessels seeking shelter in Blackhead Bay, and that it would be necessary to have another light on Blacksod Point. Nothing further was done until early in 1857, when the Board of Trade queried the need for lights at Galley Head, Fose Rocks (Blasket Islands), Bull Rock and Blackrock. The Inspecting Committee made a full report, and in its reply, the Board of Trade stated that Blackrock, of the four stations, was the most important. Trinity House duly gave statutory sanction for Blackrock.

Delay was experienced in obtaining legal possession of the rock, but by spring 1858, tenders for building the lighthouse and dwelling had been received, and the quote of £11,330 by Burgess and Sons, Limerick was accepted. Unfortunately, due to weather conditions, neither the lantern nor the apparatus could be landed on the rock in November 1862, so were stored in Belmullet until the following summer, when they were safely landed.

The circular tower – 15 metres high – is positioned on the western extremity of Blackrock. The light – 85 metres above high water, visible for 22 nautical miles, and flashing white to sea and red to land once every 30 seconds – was first exhibited on 1 June 1864. The tower, lantern and dome were painted white. The total cost – for building and the light – was £20,672.

On 20 August 1940, lantern panes and roofs were damaged by gunfire from a German bomber attacking the SS *Macville*, close to the rock. Fortunately, the keepers were unhurt. Dwellings for the keepers were built at Blacksod, and the rock became relieving in early 1893.

Blackrock was my first rock station. It was also almost my last. The principal keeper there took an instant dislike to me, and naturally the feeling was reciprocated. I have no idea why it should have been so, as we had never met and were not likely to meet very often afterwards. I had my own quarters on the rock, and the other two keepers would come in to play cards for a bit of fun. For obvious reasons, no one ever plays cards on lighthouses for money. Yet the principal keeper soon put a stop to our fun. Some of the principal keepers in those days were really feared – their word was law, and they always had the backing of the 'powers that be'. In an effort to maintain harmonious relationships at the station, none of the other keepers would dare question the principal keeper about anything. This particular principal keeper was dark, dour and unrelenting, and forbade noise or gaiety of any description. The place was like a morgue, and my radio – although subdued – was anathema to him. As a matter of fact, everything I did seemed to annoy him. Gradually, I saw less and less of my near neighbours, and became

Blackrock, Mayo

something of a 'leper'. If the principal keeper did not like me, no one else dared to; I would soon be gone, but they would have to suffer him for years ahead.

I had brought my first fishing rod to the rock, and envisaged catching all kinds of exotic fish. But despite countless hours and the use of every imaginable kind of bait, I never got a bite. The principal keeper – my arch enemy – never came back without a fish, and he would deliberately stroll by my window, swinging his fish and whistling smugly to himself. I would willingly have given at least a left arm to have something to show for my endeavours. I even used to spy out his fishing spots, but – try as I would – I never did catch a fish off that rock.

I think they must have been the longest five weeks (we were overdue three weeks) of my life, and when I did eventually get ashore, I intended to go straight home and out of the job for good. Wiser heads prevailed, and Blackrock is now just another of the very few black spots on my itinerary around the coast. I never found out why that keeper hated me so much. I met him years afterwards, and he genuinely did not remember me. Perhaps he was one of the few keepers totally unsuited to the life of a lightkeeper, and was only in the job as a successor to his forebears. *Fl WR 12s*

Broadhaven

Broadhaven

This is a harbour light tucked up on Gubbacashel Point. Unlike its neighbour around the corner on Eagle Island, it enjoys comparative peace as it guides vessels clear of hidden rock on the western side of Broadhaven, and into a safe anchorage. It was originally meant to be a beacon tower, but pressure from the locals resulted in the lighthouse that stands there today. About 9 miles from Belmullet, some of the best fishing grounds on the coast, the Stags, are close by.

The light was first exhibited in June 1885. At 25 metres above high water, it's visible for 12 nautical miles. It shows white to seaward and the east side of the haven, and red to the west. The cost, in 1885, was the not inconsiderable sum of £6,976, but this also included the dwelling and outhouse for the keeper. It became an unwatched light in 1931, and the attendant now lives in the village. The dwelling has been allowed to run down over the years – a pity, as a more peaceful and tranquil spot would be hard to find.

Belmullet was and still is our abode when visiting Broadhaven. That town, I can safely say, has to be the best market town in Ireland, with its huge catchment area from Ballina to Blacksod. A wide-open town where almost anything goes, there was never trouble getting drink at any time of the day or night, and the fair days there were a revelation. It was as if a gold rush hit the town, only this gold left an enduring smell. The fair started around five-thirty in the morning, and they were still buying and selling at midnight. It was also the home of poker in the west of Ireland. One house in particular, a licensed premises, was for many years the venue for some real action. Whole businesses came and went, and though I always got out when the going got tough, I often stayed up all night, intrigued by the consummate ease with which a small fortune could be won or – more often – lost. I remember one Sunday morning following an all-night session when the game became so intense that one of the players – a local clergyman – had to be reminded to say Mass. When the service was over, he immediately returned to carry on the play. Yes, a fine town, and it had its share of lovely girls, too. ✳ *Iso WR 4s*

Eagle Island

Two towers were constructed on Eagle Island in 1835, in addition to a massive storm wall built on the sea side of the towers. The towers – one 20 metres high, the other 25 metres high – were 260 metres apart, with their lanterns at the same level of 68 metres above high water. Built of cut stone from quarries on the island, they were painted white and their fixed white lights – visible for 20 nautical miles in clear weather – were first exhibited on the night of 29 December. When the two lights at night or the towers in daytime were in line, they guided vessels past all dangers from Blacksod Bay to Broadhaven, including the Stags.

Eagle Island seemed destined to be continually struck by severe storms. On the night of 17 January 1836, the lantern of the west tower was struck by a rock, shattering one of the panes of glass and extinguishing the light. The keepers had the light working again within an hour. The keepers' dwellings were also badly damaged. In early February 1850, both lanterns were badly damaged by a violent gale, and this time it took the keepers five days to restore the lights.

On 11 March 1861, at midday, the light room of the eastern tower was struck by the sea, smashing 23 panes. Lamps were washed down the stairs, and some of the damaged reflectors were beyond repair. It must have been a powerful wave to have come up over 40 metres of rock and a further 35 metres of lighthouse tower, and then to cause so much damage. By the following day, the keepers had restored the light, though with only twelve lamps and reflectors. An incredible consequence of this disaster was that so much water had cascaded down the tower that the keepers on the island found it impossible to open the door. Holes had to be drilled in the door to let the water out!

On Friday 29 December 1894, the east station on Eagle Island was wrecked by what must have been one of the worst storms ever to hit the west coast of Ireland. This was in the days when keepers and their families lived on the rock stations. Mr F.J. Ryan (a past principal keeper at Eagle Island) has very kindly sent me copies of letters written by two aunts who were at the east station at the time. One letter is from Polly Ryan to her sister Kate. Their father was on the Fastnet at the time, and

Kate was living ashore with her mother at the Rock Island dwellings. Polly and her other sister, Lizzy, were on Eagle Island with their brother, Tom Ryan. Tom was the father of F.J. Ryan, retired principal keeper (now living in Kinsale), and Polly later became Mrs Loughrey, mother of N.J. Loughrey – one-time principal keeper at Ferris Point, Larne Harbour – and Michael Loughrey, retired light-ship man. The Lavelle mentioned in the letter below was attached to the west lighthouse and was an uncle of a previous principal keeper, Jim Lavelle, who was afterwards attendant for many years at Tarbert lighthouse. In Lizzy's letter, she mentions Peter and Bill, sons of Lavelle and living on the rock at the time. Corish is an old service name, and very likely some of the young children on the rock that night later joined the service themselves. The eldest was Eddie, twelve years of age at the time. Lizzy's letter also mentions Anthony – in connection with the relief boat – and it is fairly certain he was a Gallagher whose family was still carrying out the reliefs until the helicopter took over. The 'Alderman' mentioned in the second paragraph is the rock outside Crookhaven, in west Cork.

Eagle Island East
Belmullet.
January 1st 1895

My dear Kate,

I trust you may all spend a joyous New Year and that you are all well. I hope that Father is safe on the rock. I trust in God nothing is wrong, as God help us poor sinners. If you knew how we put in the time you would feel for us. I told you of the gale on Friday last so I need not mention it. But Friday the 29th beats all. What would you think at half past two to jump out of bed and into water?

Well, it was blowing a terrible gale all night but we never expected anything like what occurred. The Green Seas were going over our houses as fast as if we were on the Alderman. You can imagine when we got up to see the door broken down, and the rooms all filled with the sea. My Lord, how we were, the roof being stripped of every slate and the sea raging outside, the Lantern was out.

Tom ran to Mr Corish, leaving Lizzy and I to dress ourselves, and they ran between sea, slates and all sorts. They got up and saw a pane broken in the lantern, they put in a blind pane by a hard struggle, the gale raging to its height at the time. When they came down, they came in to us and we in a mad state with fright. My God, how we were I can never tell.

However, we thought it best to be all together as window frames, roofs and all the house was going in pieces. We went in to Mrs Corish and we were all in a state waiting every moment to see what might turn up. The slates were being lifted off like flies. The youngsters were all brought downstairs, as the sea was coming down on their beds, and lucky they were, for had they remained there, killed they would have been.

All of us were sitting in Mrs Corish's room when the sea ran over the house smashing the door in the hall, filling the rooms where we had been sitting. You never saw such a sight. There we were next to mad men, while Tom and Mr Corish barred the door and swept the sea out.

Well, what can I say only we were waiting for our last moment, and poor Mrs Corish in a state and no wonder, fearful for her little ones, but they were good little dears. I, for my part, had good courage and as we were saying beforehand, never surrender, but alas, when I said that on the surface without the care of anyone but God alone to save us, I broke down. Tom gave us a telling off, told us to trust more than that in ourselves. So we tried to brave it, as pen nor paper could ever tell of our escape.

Well, as our house was said to be the best, we thought it might be better to get in if a chance offered, as the fire was put where we were sitting, by the sea coming down the chimney – a nice sight.

Dear Kate, I can never explain to you how we got on. However, you can picture us in a state like that. We had not long been in our Ship when in came the door, running into the room where we sat. Well, to try and get ourselves saved was to try and do our best. Poor Mr Corish, the likes of him I never saw. He deserves more praise than we can ever give him. Mrs Corish was brave until, after a bit, the poor woman she was very much shocked. As any woman would be to see her little family there. We were praying for the Lord to lessen the gale, but no sign of it getting any better. We were in an awful state all night trying to bar the sea out.

Well, Mr Corish's place got all broken down, upstairs got knocked into one. The windows all broken in, the staircase carried away, I can't tell you, Lizzy, I dare say Tom will give you particulars correct. We cleared out to our place as we don't know how it might be with us. God alone knows how we were saved.

The lights were put out several times, all the panes in the Tower window were put in. They went to have a look and the paint and oil stores were levelled to the ground, pantries and everything smashed. Flags were torn up and tossed round like marbles. Nobody would realise it only us that had seen it.

Our suffering was terrible. My Lord to see the sea breaking over us tearing all away and no chance of escape, we all expected to be in the other World before now. Tom and Mr Corish would try and be gay, but only deceiving was in their hearts. They thought, as they told us since, that carried away we would be in the morning.

The men from the Upper Station came down between the sprays, and we were saying they were likely carried away as their station is said to be the most exposed, but they had not suffered much. Of course, all the outhouses were wrecked. They came and took us one by one to their station, to Mrs Callaghan and Lavelles and we were thankful to God to reach them. All things were destroyed on Mrs Corish. My God, such a wreck you have never seen. They took all things of any account to this station where we all remain awaiting orders. Flags were put up yesterday, and the boat came today. It's gone since with Telegrams to the Office for fresh water and salt.

Lizzy, Tom and I, Mr and Mrs Corish and some of the young-sters are in Mrs Callaghan's. Mrs Doran, Mrs Corish's aunt, and a few youngsters were in Mrs Lavelle's. Such a state you have never seen any place in. Everywhere levelled, but we were thank-ful to God for our escape. Our good neighbours deserve credit for the attention, I must say. So long, trusting in God dear Father is all right, as the likes of the gale we have never seen. Mother is well I hope. Write soon. I will write again when the boat will be out.

You little think how we are today, the Lower Station is a com-plete wreck.

Good luck,

Polly

P.S. You will excuse this as the men must get dinner. They are going mad, running joyously at our escape. Lizzy will tell you all.

Good-bye,

Your loving sister Polly

Eagle Island

Following this episode, shore dwellings for the keepers and their families were built at Corclough on the Termoncarragh road, near to where keepers could semaphore to the island. The families moved into dwellings towards the end of 1900.

An additional navigational aid – a radio beacon – was established on 21 January 1937. This beacon sent out a Morse signal – G.L. – every 6 minutes in conjunction with five other radio-beacon stations – two in Ireland, and the other three in Scotland, the Scilly Isles and France. Thus, a continuous service on a selected frequency could be picked up by a vessel, and its position could be determined on a chart from two or three bearings obtained from these stations. The light was converted to electricity on 17 July 1968, when the candle power was increased to 1,400,000. The light can be seen for 26 nautical miles.

Reliefs were for a long time carried out by a private contractor's boat from Scotchport, 2 miles south of the island on the Mullet. Later, when the helicopter took over, the keepers were landed at Blacksod.

✴ *Fl (3) W 10s* *

Blackrock, Sligo

Originally, there were no less than seven lights located at the mouth of Sligo Harbour. When one considers the almost constant silting up of its entrance, it would seem that all seven were justified. A beacon had been established on Blackrock, Sligo some time in the eighteenth century. At some point, it was washed away, and by 1814, the merchants of Sligo were looking to have the beacon re-established. The work carried out by a local man in 1816 was found to be inadequate, so a more substantial beacon of limestone was built by Thomas Ham of Ballina. Completed in November 1819, it was 15.5 metres high.

During 1821, ship owners of Sligo requested that the Blackrock beacon be converted to a lighthouse, and that a 'metal man' be placed on a pedestal on Perch Rock, off Oyster Island. The 'metal man' took up his position, but the Blackrock beacon was not converted to a lighthouse until 1833–34. Then, using the solid beacon as a base, an outside spiral staircase led to the entrance door well above the high-water mark. The light was established on 1 June 1835, and panniers were added in 1863 to allow for extra accommodation. The light was converted from oil to acetylene and made unwatched, and the lantern truncated on 29 November 1934. A further conversion – to electricity – took place on 15 September 1965. An auxiliary light was established over the Wheaten and Seal rocks on 1 December 1891, but discontinued on 11 November 1893, when a red sector was introduced to the main light. This was discontinued in 1898, and the auxiliary re-established. Like the main light, the auxiliary was converted to electricity on 15 September 1965. ✳ *Fl W 5s*

Oyster Island

I lived for many periods in our quarters on Oyster, and I suppose the most frustrating part was its closeness to Rosses Point. Just across the narrow channel was the dance hall attached to The Elsinore – a pub-cum-guest house at the aptly named Memory Harbour – and the music and laughter sounded tantalisingly close on the island. The principal keeper and his assistant kept a boat, but the channel, though very narrow, was extremely dangerous. Many a time in daylight I tried to row across,

Oyster Island

only to find the fierce current taking me way off course. Indeed, the same channel has claimed many lives in recent years. As we will see below, I was one of the lucky ones, having once tried to swim it.

Two lights were established on 1 August 1837, forming leading lights from Sligo Bay into the channel to Sligo Port. When they ceased to give an accurate lead, they were discontinued and replaced by a sectored, temporary light on 15 February 1891. By February 1893, the two discontinued towers had been taken down, and the north tower was being rebuilt towards the north-west point of Oyster Island. It became a rear leading light with the 'metal man' in 1932. The light was converted from acetylene to propane gas on 9 October 1979. *Oc W 4s*

'Metal Man', Sligo

'Metal man', Sligo

The Sligo 'metal man' – an identical twin of his counterpart in Tramore, County Waterford – was initially intended to be placed on the Blackrock beacon, but when the merchants of Sligo looked for Blackrock to be converted to a lighthouse, the 'sailor' – in 1821 and at their suggestion – was placed on Perch Rock. An acetylene light was later established beside him, and he was converted to propane gas on 9 October 1979.

I mentioned earlier my foolhardy efforts to swim the channel, but on one very memorable occasion, I found myself immersed involuntarily in that same channel. It was a blustery day in June 1964 as we edged our way out to the 'metal man'. The tide was on the turn, and soon the area around the base of the structure would be dried out. It had been reported that the character of the light was erratic, necessitating the installation of a new flashing unit. The boatman, with some difficulty, was tying the boat to the ladder at the side of the 'metal man', but already I was on my way up the ladder, climbing with one hand and holding the flasher with the other. Even after all these years, I still find it hard to believe what happened next. All I do know is that I missed the top rung of the ladder by a fraction of an inch (it might as well have been a mile), and suddenly I was plunging backwards with mouth open into the depths of the sea. How I missed the bow of the boat on the way down is still a mystery, as it was tied to the ladder. This was no ordinary sea, but a mad, rushing tide, hell-bent on going its own hectic course. I was soon on my way towards the middle of the channel, though this is something I learnt later – by then, I was unconscious. I floated rapidly, face downwards, away from the boat, as the men made frantic efforts to untie it and get the engine going. Then, inexplicably, I began to float in the opposite direction. Fortunately for me, they were experienced seamen, and though life jackets were non-existent in those days, they had in the boat that very valuable piece of equipment, a boat-hook. They told me afterwards that I cheated death, as they reckoned I was all of 7 minutes under the water. The men fished me out, placed me over a seat and pumped the water out of me. When they eventually got me ashore and into The Elsinore, someone rang the office in Dublin. The first question asked was if the light was working and where was their precious flasher. That's the worst of being expendable. ✳ *Fl W 4s* ✳

Lower Rosses

Lower Rosses

This is Yeats country, of course. William and his brother, Jack, spent much of their childhood with their grandparents in this part of Sligo. Jack captured on canvas one of their childhood memories of bathing at Rosses Point, and said that in every picture he painted there was a thought of Sligo.

The light here, established as a lighted beacon on 16 October 1908, was constructed on timber piles in the sand off Lower Rosses. Like the 'metal man' and Oyster Island, it was converted from acetylene to propane on 9 October 1979. ✳ *Fl (2) WRG 10s* ✳

St John's Point, Donegal

On the way towards the north-west coast, pay a quiet visit to St John's Point. Actually, there are two lighthouses bearing this name – the other is in County Down. This one, designed by George Halpin and established in 1832, consists of a white tower, 15 metres high, its light 30 metres above sea level with a range of 14 miles. There is a lovely description of it in *The Cliff-scenery of South-western Donegal* by Kinnfaela (T.C. McGinley), published in 1867:

the front yard, beautifully paved with fine brown sandstone . . . [is] kept at all times scrupulously clean. In this yard stands the lighthouse, a lofty circular tower, with a balcony round it near the top, and roofed in dome-like form. The walls near the top supporting the dome consist of large plates of glass, through which the blaze from the reflectors within are transmitted in all directions.

It is not long since I visited the Donegal station; about 9 miles from the village of Dunkineely, it is approached by a scenic and sandy route, a road that was often impassable due to sand and sea encroachment. That problem has now been resolved, but the visitor has still to be wary as it is a narrow road, and the magnificent terrain is inclined to divert one's attention.

St John's is another of those extremely lonely outposts. A family named Byrne tended this light for a longer period than any other on the coast. Regrettably, the attendant, Paddy Byrne, is no longer with us, but his widow, Susan (who had to move out of the lighthouse dwelling to make way for the new attendant), is still living locally. She now dwells in an ultra-modern bungalow perched high on the side of a hill, with an uninterrupted panoramic view of the whole of Donegal Bay. I stayed with her the last time I was visiting the lighthouse, and we spent many a night recalling old times at the station. She has a prodigious memory, and is able to recall people and events I have long forgotten. Susan lived in isolation for many years, with just her family to attend to, and every official visitor must have been a major distraction from everyday lighthouse chores. When the Byrnes lived at the lighthouse, our personnel always stayed there, and Susan usually did the cooking for us. The children, long since adults, have moved away. Susan now sits by her window in her hill-top home, knitting away the hours, always happy to meet people from the past. ✳ *Fl W 6s*

Rotten Island

What a name to give to that lovely, quiet island just outside Killybegs Harbour, and to the location of a lighthouse which must be of inestimable value to the multimillion-pound trawlers which pass nightly under her beams. Once again the work of George Halpin, it was established in 1838. Tragically, three workers drowned during construction. Built with cut granite, it was painted white on completion. The light underwent several changes, and it was only when converted to electricity in 1963 that it was considered an adequate light. From 2,600 candelas, electricity enabled an increase in power to 13,000 candelas in the white sector, and 2,600 in the red. The white sector has a range of 15 nautical miles, while the red's range is 11 miles.

Many times, when we had our quarters on the island, I would watch the trawlers filing past the island, for all the world like a never-ending

Rotten Island

train, their multicoloured lights intermittently blacked out by enormous flocks of seagulls screeching mercilessly for the entrails of the disembowelled fish.

Alas, like most of our other small-island stations around the coast, no one lives on Rotten Island now, though the attendant can maintain a constant vigil by means of a strategically cut-out viewpoint in the lantern, quite visible from his vantage point ashore. ✳*Fl WR 4s*

Rathlin O'Birne

This lighthouse is probably better known to fishermen from the major fishing ports of Greencastle and Killybegs than any other on the coast. The proposal to automate it around 1975 was met with a justified outcry, but by then it had been chosen to become our first and possibly the most powerful nuclear lighthouse in the world.

The first light exhibited on this tower appeared on 4 April 1856, and showed a flashing white light seaward and a red light towards land. The circular limestone tower is 20 metres high, and the light is 30 metres above high water. Originally, the lantern and dome were painted red, but in 1935, the whole tower was painted white. The light exhibited from this tower for many years emanated from a circular, six-wick burner inside a revolving dioptric lens. In 1908, this was replaced by a paraffin-vapour burner. The keepers lived in two houses on the rock, and Glencolmcille was chosen for the dwellings for their families ashore.

The idea for a nuclear lighthouse first arose in 1964, when Irish Lights was asked for its view on isotope-powered thermo-electric generators in the maritime lighting and navigational field. Blackrock, Mayo was first selected as the site for this innovation, but technical obstacles ruled it out – primarily due to the light being 90 metres above sea level. So

Rathlin O'Birne

Rathlin O'Birne was chosen for the experiment. The isotope generator was dispatched from Harwell in England, and landed on the rock on 7 June 1974. Temporary lights were erected on the balcony of the tower during the changeover, and were in use up to 15 August. On that night, the first nuclear light came into operation, flashing white and red every 20 seconds, with a range of 22 nautical miles for the white light, and 18 nautical miles for the red sector. If, for any reason, the main light failed, two standby lanterns on the tower balcony came into use. It was calculated that the output of the nuclear-powered generator would last a maximum of ten years, by which time it would have insufficient power to keep the light functioning at full strength. Ironically, when this nuclear period elapsed, two ordinary wind generators were set up, and worked very successfully until 1994, when yet another change took place. Now, power on Rathlin O'Birne is obtained from a batch of solar panels.

When the light became automatic and the keepers were withdrawn in September 1974, the station became the responsibility of a local attendant. From his shore base, he could simply press a button and be kept fully informed by radio link of any discrepancy in the lighthouse equipment. By a strange coincidence, the keepers were not too long off the rock when two tragedies took place in the treacherous waters around the lighthouse. Two Donegal trawlers – the *Evelyn Marie* and the *Carraig Nua* – were wrecked, with the loss of eleven lives. It is highly unlikely that a manned lighthouse would have averted these tragedies, but the nagging doubt remains, especially with Donegal fishermen.

Aranmore

Strangely enough, despite the absence of any important commercial traffic, Donegal boasts several major lighthouses. The one on Aranmore Island is reached by boat from Burtonport. This lovely little fishing harbour is utterly confined, and a confusing anchorage for fishing and pleasure craft of all sizes and shapes. At any given time, these boats can be six deep on the quay wall, and some skill is needed to get onto an outside boat. There are hourly trips to the island, and in recent years, a regular ferry service has been added.

It is probably this easy access that, for me anyway, takes from Aranmore much of the glamour of island life. Then again, it's a modern island, differing totally from Tory or Rathlin. On Aranmore, life is as normal as living ashore. Hotels, pubs and guest houses abound, and it is really no different from the more accessible places. At the lighthouse, however, the situation is entirely different, and this must be one of the loneliest of its kind. I honestly believe that very few visitors to the island know of its existence, yet it exhibits one of the most powerful lights on the coast, and the structure is an impressive one. From its balcony, I could never detect any human habitation. It is like being on an isolated rock like Fastnet or Tearaght, but at least on such places one never expects company. A big event was the arrival of the postman – not a regular occurrence, and who could blame him? It would be hard to equal the potholes on the road to the lighthouse.

Aranmore was only a two-man station, and many a keeper must have kept a decidedly lonesome watch when his fellow keeper had to go to the village for provisions. This meant a walk of 7 miles, and with 'interruptions' and so on, this journey could take a long time. The only redeeming feature for me on Aranmore was the presence, near the lighthouse, of a rainbow-trout lake (one of the few in Ireland). I have spent many a pleasant hour there trying to catch these elusive creatures.

The first lighthouse on Aranmore – at 14 metres high and 62 metres above sea level – was completed in 1798 by Thomas Rogers. In 1810, the lighthouse came under the control of the Port of Dublin Corporation, and considerable improvements were made to the light during the period 1817–24. When the lighthouse on Tory Island was established in 1832, the light on Aranmore was discontinued, despite protests from mariners using those waters. The protests never subsided, and eventually – in 1859, and on receipt of numerous requests from masters and ship owners – approval was granted for the re-establishment of the Aranmore light. A new, 23-metre tower, designed by George Halpin, was constructed by Messrs Daniel Crowe and Sons of Dublin. Masonry from the old tower and dwellings was partly used in the construction of the new station. The cast-iron lantern and balcony were supplied by Messrs Edmundson of Dublin. The second-order optic apparatus, which had been removed from Rathlin O'Birne in 1864, was used at Aranmore. The light, established on 1 February 1864, is 71 metres above high water.

Not long after its establishment, a captain with Anchor Line Packets

– a Glasgow shipping company – pointed out the similarity of character between Aranmore and Skerryvore lighthouses, and the danger that ships might mistake the two. This was investigated in 1874, and a new light was recommended in 1875. Approval was granted by Trinity House, and the new light was lit for the first time on 1 April 1877, flashing white and red alternately every 20 seconds. A fixed, red auxiliary light was also established in 1877 to shine over the Stags Rocks, which lie northeast of the lighthouse. This became a fixed, white light in 1904.

During the period 1924–26, considerable discussion took place about the desirability of a fog signal at Aranmore. Both diaphone and explosive-type fog signals were considered, but the Board of Trade decided

Aranmore

not to proceed. A proposal in 1927 to improve the light also failed to receive support. In 1949, improvement of the light was again mooted, and approval was granted in 1950 for conversion of the light to electricity, with an improved range of 29 nautical miles. The auxiliary light was also converted at that time. The character of the main light was altered to two white flashes every 20 seconds. ESB mains became available on Aranmore in the late 1960s, and a mains supply was connected to the lighthouse in 1970. Conversion of the light to automatic operation took place in 1976, and the keepers were withdrawn on 1 August 1976. The attendant lives in the village of Leabgarrow, a distance of 5 kilometres from the lighthouse. A remote monitoring system keeps him informed of conditions at the lighthouse. The auxiliary light was altered from flashing white to flashing red on 1 April 1982.

✳ Fl (2) W 20s · Auxiliary: Fl R 3s

Ballagh Rocks

Ballagh Rocks, or Carraig na Bealach (the 'road rock'), is at the northern end of the channel of water between Aranmore Island and the Donegal mainland village of Burtonport. The stretch of water is also known as the 'Aranmore Roads'. Ballagh Rocks is the largest of a group of rocks known collectively as Blackrocks.

A beacon on the rocks was completed in 1875, and considered by mariners to be of great assistance to navigation. The conical-shaped stone beacon is approximately 4.5 metres in diameter by 9 metres high. In 1980, it was decided to place a light on the beacon, and work went ahead in constructing a landing together with a lean-to hut against the beacon for propane gas bottles and equipment, an access ladder to the lantern on top of the beacon and a pathway from the landing to the beacon.

Early in June 1981, the contract Bolkow 105 helicopter, EI–BDI, ditched while conveying an underslung skip of concrete; the helicopter was flying between Arlands Point and Ballagh Rocks. Fortunately, the pilot managed to get clear of the sinking helicopter and swam to nearby rocks, where he was picked up by the attending boat at Ballagh Rocks and taken to Burtonport.

Though a Notice to Mariners was issued in July 1981, severe conditions meant the lantern could not be fitted to the top of the beacon until 21 May 1982 – nine months later than intended. The character is a 1-second white flash every 2.5 seconds.

It could be said that an enforced stay of mine in Burtonport was probably the direct cause of that light now being electric. Ballagh Rocks is virtually impossible to land on most of the time; in 1983, I spent a month in Burtonport trying to get there to effect emergency repairs. So it was decided to install long-life batteries instead, and to remove the propane apparatus. This was done on 1 May 1983, and the light has since worked satisfactorily. ✳ *Fl W 2.5s*

Northern Lights ✸

Tory Island

Tory is literally as old as the hills. Neolithic farmers colonised this island several thousand years ago, and though very little trace of that period now remains, it is said that the perimeter wall surrounding the lighthouse is built from stone from the only remaining building of that era. I pride myself in knowing a smattering of our national language, but that Tory dialect had me completely baffled. Even after several visits to that island, I never could understand one word of Tory Irish; I could only go by signs and intuition.

The boat trip to Tory was, and still is, one of the longest and most difficult to any of our islands. The island is our most north-westerly one, lying as it does about 8 miles off Bloody Foreland. Great Atlantic seas, combined with treacherous currents, are a constant menace, and it is only in latter years that the acquisition of larger boats has somewhat eased the passage to the island. My first trip to Tory had a touch of the tragicomedy about it. I was a bad sailor in my early days with Irish Lights, and I had been stranded ashore in Bunbeg for a week, awaiting passage, when the contractor decided to take advantage of a half-suitable day and make the trip. The boat was loaded with enough provisions to feed an army, and it was made quite plain to me that supplying the natives was a lot more important than getting me to my lighthouse. But after only half an hour afloat, there was no mistaking the last gasp of the old inboard engine before she gave up and died. By this time, I was lying in a prone position over the gunwale, my head not very far from the green seas. What made it all the more embarrassing was the obvious contentment of the old people aboard and their enjoyment of the trip – to them, of course, it was second nature, and they seemed not to mind the deadly exhaust fumes wafting into the boat, and the deteriorating weather and sea conditions. As frantic efforts were being made to restart the engine, I spied a few curious glances in my direction and a garbled 'engineer' being mentioned. Deciding discretion to be the better part of valour, I leaned even further over the side and made a herculean effort to throw up what was left inside me, which was not a lot. And even in the whole of my health, I honestly would not have known one end of that antique engine from the other. But just as it seemed my face-saving effort was in vain, and movements were being made in my direction, the old engine suddenly spluttered to life, and we were on our way again. Though I have improved as a sailor over the years, I am still very glad that any trip I may now make to Tory, albeit for pleasure, will be by helicopter.

I like Tory Island and I like its people. I believe they are the poorest, proudest and most genuine of any of our island folk. While I would love to see it more publicised and visited by discerning people, I dearly wish that it will never become another Inishmore. While not decrying the latter in any way, I do believe it to be vastly over-commercialised and to have suffered because of that. Tory, fortunately or otherwise, is so hard to reach that there is no danger of its becoming just another island.

It is not my purpose to dwell on Tory, as it really deserves a book all to itself, but it would be almost impossible to isolate one from the other, as the lighthouse and its people have for years formed an integral part of life on the island. On my first night at the lighthouse, while taking a stroll outside the compound, I noticed a lot of cans and jars placed in strategic positions around the outside of the lighthouse compound. The next morning these had all disappeared, and it was not long before I discovered that this was one of the local 'barter' systems operational then. Apparently, surplus paraffin was being exchanged, but for what I never found out, as the islanders could ill afford to return the favour. Maybe this was a genuine giveaway on the part of the lightkeepers, but if so, it was unique, as they were never known on the coast for their philanthropic ways. In any case, this surplus oil would be from a consignment of paraffin that would have been deemed unsuitable for the high standard required to keep the incandescent burner and the main light functioning correctly. This oil, however, could still be used successfully for house lamps and cooking stoves.

The contrast between the affluent lifestyle of the lighthouse staff at the station and that of the islanders was very obvious. The lighthouse was always amply stocked with fuel, coal and provisions, and eventually had its own helicopter relief. By comparison, the once-fertile land on Tory has been all but destroyed by the constant stripping of surface scraws as replacement fuel for the turf which has long since disappeared. Farming is practically non-existent, and the breadwinners divide their time between labouring in Britain – mainly Scotland – and the lucrative lobster and salmon season at home.

Tory has many attractions, and its ever-changing moods have been successfully captured by a few local artists. That superb painter, Derek Hill, filled many canvases during his sojourns on the island. He used a little hut near the lighthouse as his habitat when there.

I was never bored on Tory. On my first visit, this might have been due to the presence of an émigrée returned from Scotland on holidays, and whom I met at a *céilí* shortly after arriving there. My proposed fortnight's stay lengthened into something like two months. There did seem to be an awful lot of work at the lighthouse that year!

The best *céilís*, and the best *céilí* dancers, are on Tory Island. The dances usually start around midnight and go on all night. One would need to be very fit to stand the pace, but I suppose the fact that most of them could sleep the next day accounted somewhat for their boundless energy.

On my second visit to Tory, an elephant was washed up on the beach midway between the lighthouse and the village. This poor creature

Tory Island

had perhaps been part of a circus being transported by sea, and had died or fallen overboard. For weeks, the smell was appalling, and following numerous entreaties by the locals, Donegal County Council sent out a load of cement to entomb the elephant on the rocky shore. When the job was done, there was still an ample supply of that commodity left over, and many half-built houses very soon became habitable!

After a long period on Tory, one could easily go native and forget the existence of the outside world. To me, it became something of a Shangri-La minus the comforts, though the absence of rent, rates or taxes must surely make for an idyllic lifestyle for the inhabitants.

I seem to have left the lighthouse until last. This light was requested by the Harbour Commissioners and merchants of Sligo in April 1828. Approval for the project was granted by the Ballast Board in November, and statutory sanction was received from Trinity House in December 1828. At this early stage, it was decided that when Tory Island light was established, Aranmore light would be extinguished. The tower and buildings were designed by Inspector George Halpin, and built by the workmen of the Board under his supervision.

The light was established on 1 August 1832. The tower is 27 metres high and the light 40 metres above sea level. A dioptric lens with multi-wick oil lamp replaced the original oil lamps and reflectors in 1862. A major alteration was made to the optic in 1887. The lens revolved, thereby giving a flashing character, and the light source was coal gas, which lasted until 1923. Gas was made in the gasworks at the station. A fog signal was established in 1887, and the radio beacon in 1931. From 1923 to 1972, the light source was vaporised paraffin. In 1972, the lighthouse was electrified. ✳ *Fl (4) W 30s* ✳

Fanad Head

Making our way along the north-east coast, we arrive at Fanad Head lighthouse, at the entrance to Lough Swilly. Close to the town of Milford, Irish Lights maintains a helicopter here for reliefs to Inishtrahull and Tory Island. The only thing of note I remember about Fanad is that, while there, I came close – for the only time – to not getting home at Christmas. That sounds rather odd for a land station, but that year we had been snowed under for two weeks, and it was only on Christmas Eve that a path could be cleared through to the lighthouse, which enabled transport to operate and facilitated my belated but joyous homecoming.

Fanad Head light is classified as a sea light, as distinct from a harbour light, although it does mark the entrance to Lough Swilly, which forms a natural harbour of refuge. In 1812, the frigate *Saldana* was wrecked on Fannet Point – as it was called in those days – and was a complete loss except for the ship's parrot, which bore a silver collar inscribed

'Saldana'. Soon after the loss of this vessel, Captain Hill of the Royal Navy in Derry, whose experience of the north-west coast from Blacksod to Lough Foyle was second to none, wrote to one of the members of the Board suggesting that a lighthouse be placed on Fannet Point. He backed up his request by stating that the *Saldana* would not have been lost if there had been a light on Fannet. Without further ado, the Board approved Captain Hill's request, and approached Trinity House, which gave its approval in July 1814. Designed by the Corporation's inspector, George Halpin, building was undertaken by the Ballast Board's workmen. The Admiralty signal tower on Fannet was taken over, ostensibly so as to be used as a keeper's dwelling and to prevent local inhabitants from dismantling it for their own devices. In fact, it seems to have been taken down by the Corporation, and its stone used when the lighthouse and dwellings were built.

The first lighthouse was similar in size to two other towers being built

Fanad Head

around the same time – one at Mutton Island off Salthill, Galway and the other at Roches Point at the eastern entrance to Cork Harbour. Each had an inside diameter of 178 centimetres, and was three storeys high – ground, first floor and lantern. Fannet Point was first lit on 18 March 1817, and its fixed, non-flashing light showed red to sea and white towards the lough. It could be seen for 14 nautical miles in clear water. The optic consisted of nine Argand sperm-oil wick lamps and parabolic reflectors. The seaward lamps would have had red-coloured lamp glasses.

A new and larger tower was later built close to the original one, and this light went into operation in 1886. The incandescent apparatus was installed in 1909, and was in use until 1975, when the light was converted to unwatched electric – that is, the night watch was discontinued. The light character was also altered, from group flashing, six, white and red, to group flashing, five, white and red. The auxiliary light over the Limeburner Rock was discontinued in 1977, and replaced by another red sector in the main light; the other red sector is over the Swilly Rocks.

Perhaps one of the most revolutionary changes to occur in the lighthouse service took place towards the end of 1969, when helicopters were introduced to effect the relief of rock stations from Fastnet in the southwest to Inishtrahull on the north coast. Fanad Head was chosen as the land base for Tory Island and Inishtrahull, and what could be at times, especially for Tory, hours in a boat in choppy seas from Bunbeg is now a matter of minutes in comparative comfort. ✳*Fl (5) WR 20s*

Dunree

Dunree is located in a similar situation to the light at Charlesfort in Kinsale. In common with Charlesfort, its surrounding fort is being restored to something like its original state. At one time, the only lighthouse in the immediate vicinity of Lough Swilly was Fanad Head, but in March 1871, the Duke of Abercorn backed up numerous signatories in a memorial to the Commissioners which sought better lighting for the Lough. The duke suggested converting the two Martello towers at Macanish and Dunree. The government, however, made it clear it had no intention of disposing of the towers. During 1872, representatives of Trinity House came over to investigate, and agreed that lights should be established at Dunree Head and on Buncrana pier. The Board of Trade concurred with Trinity House. The Inspecting Committee surveyed the site, and reported that the fort at Dunree was not a suitable position for the new lighthouse. It suggested a position on higher ground to the north, in which case the tower would not have to be more than one-storey high. Work went ahead, and a lantern, attached to a dwelling for the keeper, was designed and built by Messrs McClelland and Company of Derry. The optic was supplied by Chance Brothers of Birmingham. When the light was established on 15 January 1876, its light was fixed, non-flashing, with a two-wick burner using oil in a 500-millimetre-diameter lens. The lantern is at ground level, attached to and in front of the dwelling. The light is 46 metres above high water. The character now is flashing, two, white, red, 5 seconds. The range is white 12 nautical miles, red 9 nautical miles. Candle power is white 5,000, red 1,200. The structure is 6 metres in height. On 9 December 1927, the light was converted to unwatched acetylene with a carbide-generating plant attached to the station. A group of seven acetylene burners replaced the wick lamp, and the fixed light became flashing with two flashes every 5 seconds.

When the light became unwatched, the keeper – J. Murphy – was pensioned and became the attendant. The light had another conversion, this time to electricity, in June 1969, the source of illumination being a cluster of three 100-watt, 220-volt lamps. If the electricity should fail, a small, electric generator automatically takes over until mains supply

Dunree

is restored. The attendants since 1930 have been Mr H. Brennan until 1951, Mr P. Curry until 1955, and then Mr P. Redmond; his son is now the attendant. *Fl (2) WR 5s*

Buncrana

A lovely description of Buncrana as it once was – and in some respects still is – can be found in *Lewis's Topographical Dictionary of Ireland* (1837), when this market town had just over a thousand inhabitants:

> Though of some importance in the reign of Elizabeth, this place subsequently fell into great decay . . . The town is beautifully

situated on the eastern shore of Lough Swilly, at the foot of the mountains of Ennishowen, and, from the romantic and picturesque beauty and salubrity of its position, has of late years become a bathing-place of considerable resort . . . Lough Swilly here expands into an arm of the sea, bounded by mountains and rocks of majestic character, and forming a capacious haven of easy access, suitable for vessels of any burden . . . Two rivers empty themselves into the lough, one on each side of the town, after falling over several ledges of rock in their channels: in the northern, or, as it is commonly called, the Castle river, is an extensive and valuable salmon fishery; on the southern river are flax, oatmeal, and flour-mills.

The light at Buncrana was established on 15 January 1876, and was converted to acetylene from oil lamps on 4 November 1916. It was converted to electricity on 10 April 1951. The character of the light is isophase white, red, 4 seconds (2 seconds by 2 seconds). The intensity is white 12,000 candle power, red 3,000 candle power. The range is white 15 nautical miles, red 12 nautical miles. The height above high water is 8 metres, and the structure is 8 metres in height. *Iso WR 4s*

Inishtrahull

Inishtrahull lighthouse, off the Donegal coast, is the most northerly of lighthouses on our coast. The island on which it is located derives its name from Irish, and means 'the island of the big strand'. Yet apart from a large raised mound of shingle, I have never seen any evidence of sand. The island, 1 mile in length and about a third in width, has a hill at both ends with a plateau in the centre. It once supported a thriving population, and there are signs of prehistoric occupation. When the fog signal was being built on the west side of the island in the early 1900s, an oval stone inscribed with a cross was unearthed from a very deep chamber, suggesting a hiding place for its safety. There are also minute remains of a Celtic church which would have been destroyed by the Vikings in the tenth century. The island was uninhabited for many years after this Viking period, but like many other islands around the coast, actually flourished around the time of the Famine. Desperate people fled to these outposts of civilisation in the hope of finding succour from the blighted mainland. There was even a fish-curing station in Inishtrahull, the remains of which can still be seen.

It would appear from accounts I have read that the Hull (as it is known in the service) was not a lonely place on which to live. The inhabitants appeared to have had a good, if precarious, living from the few acres of land on the island, but it was from the sea that their main resources came. Turbet fishing – using conger eels for bait – seemed to be their main catch. They also got large amounts of provisions from passing boats, and no sailing vessel was allowed pass without being boarded. Rival crews often pulled out from the island, and in their efforts to arrive first at these lucrative prey, I imagine many a rowing record must have been broken in the process. The islanders would be the first strangers the captains and crews would have seen since leaving New York or Philadelphia four or five weeks earlier, and they and their fresh fruit, fowl and eggs would be very welcome. In return, the islanders received tea, sugar, black treacle and clothes, and no doubt their dire tales of poverty on the island enlarged their quotas of goodies. Bartering was made much easier by the fact that these ships, being so near their destination, had to get rid of their surplus stores, as the ships' owners would otherwise cut back on the next voyage.

The islanders brewed their own liquor, using treacle as a substitute for malt. As a result, frequent running battles seem to have been waged with the coastguards, and a constant vigil had to be kept. The island and its lifestyle took a terrible toll. The inhabitants enjoyed their time ashore, but when the money ran out, they often took off for home in the most dreadful conditions. Consequently, the death toll from drowning was high, and this unhappy ending accounted for almost all the men on the island. Happily, this fate did not befall one of our service's most colourful characters, Captain McLoughlin, born on the Hull and who commanded one of our service steamers with distinction for many years.

The first lighthouse on Inishtrahull was built by George Halpin in 1812, at the east end of the island. In 1905, when British naval ships were operating out of Lough Swilly, there was a request for a fog-signal station on the island – a request complied with by the Lighthouse Authority, which decided to build on the opposite side of the island to the lighthouse though this entailed manning two separate stations. When an inspection of the lighthouse was carried out in 1954, it was seen to be in need of major repairs, and a new tower was deemed necessary. This time, it was decided to build it on the west side of the island, and incorporate it with the fog signal. I was practically resident on the island during the building and reconstruction work, and saw between fifteen and twenty men – many of them from around Malin Head – engaged for the job. Accommodation was so limited at Inishtrahull that even a new bath waiting to be installed was put into service as a bed. We worked long, hard hours for six days a week, and on Sunday evenings, we played football in the hollow of the island. The fierce rivalry between the 'locals' and the 'visitors' was witnessed only by the rabbits and the sea birds, but I have often thought what a splendid amphitheatre this setting would be for one of our modern rock concerts.

The new lighthouse, the first to be built by Irish Lights since the beginning of the century, was completed and put into operation in 1958. This tall, slender tower – 23 metres high, and built of reinforced concrete – has a light intensity of 1.75 million candelas, with a range of 20 nautical miles. It is 59 metres above high water, and has the unusual feature of a diaphone fog signal mounted above the lantern, thereby ensuring that the powerful, air-driven signal will be heard on all sides as it completes the full arc. By an ironic twist, on the day that this latest addition to the service was being officially opened, the weather – which had been exceptionally good up to then – turned sour, and the Commissioners were left helplessly viewing their 'baby' from the deck of their flagship, *Granuaile*.

The east lighthouse was pulled down shortly after this, and all that remains is the stub of the old tower and the little graveyard just beyond it. Now that the west lighthouse has become automated, the island has once more reverted to its natural state, with the human element no more than a memory. All that remains on this island honeycombed by rabbits are the ghosts of generations of lightkeepers. ✳*Fl (3) W 15s##*

Inishowen

Inishowen lighthouse in Shrove, about 5 miles from that busy fishing port of Greencastle, was the first lighthouse I ever visited. It was mid-August, and I was in the tender care of our most senior technician, a man named Harry Bent, whose unenviable task was to initiate his protégé into the business of lighthouse maintenance. Shrove is one of our better lighthouse locations, and attracts quite a few visitors during the summer. So, irrespective of the close attention of my mentor, I decided it was not going to be all work and no play for yours truly. I was also more than a little amused at being paid for the privilege of doing just as I pleased beyond the confines of home or the scrutiny of parents.

Our quarters at the lighthouse were in the process of being renovated, so Mr Bent – as I was expected to call him – had to find accommodation locally. This was very scarce just then, and when we did eventually find a place to stay, we had to share a bed. It soon became apparent that this arrangement was going to be a disaster. I invariably arrived back in the digs in the small hours of the morning, and Harry – with the aid of a torch – would note the time on an enormous pocket watch he kept on the chair beside the bed. The following day, he would refuse to talk to me for hours, and when he eventually did, it was only to threaten to report my behaviour to a higher authority. Early one morning, on my way home with a girl from a dance in Greencastle, he passed us on his way to work and totally ignored us. Harry and I did come to an understanding later, and I probably owe him a great deal for trying to keep me on the straight and narrow at that delicate stage of my life. He also gave me a lot of

Inishowen

sound advice, some of which I like to think stood to me in later years in my meanderings around the coast.

Originally, two lighthouses were built at Dunagree Point, 1 kilometre south of Inishowen Head, and used as harbour lights to guide vessels into Lough Foyle and lead clear of the Tuns Bank. Applications for a light at the entrance to Lough Foyle were made in January and March 1832 by both the Derry Ballast Office and Derry Chamber of Commerce. The board of the Corporation for Improving the Port of Dublin instructed George Halpin to proceed to Inishowen and check the locality. Three proposals were received in May 1835 to build the two towers designed by Mr Halpin; that of Mr James Pettigrew of Dorset Street, Dublin, for £368, was selected. The two keepers' dwellings and the rest of the station were built by the workmen of the Board, again to Mr Halpin's design and under his supervision. The twin towers, bearing east and west, were of cut stone, 140 metres apart and painted white. The fixed white lights – 20.4 metres above high water – were established on 1 December 1837.

During July 1900, a Notice to Mariners was issued, stating that a siren fog signal would be established on 1 October 1900. A third, two-storey dwelling was built to accommodate the additional two assistant keepers required for fog-signal duty. Until 1912, only one was appointed. Following Inspector Dean's suggestion in November 1907 that black bands be painted around the towers to make them more conspicuous, the Inspecting Committee recommended one black band on the east tower, and two on the west. Trinity House gave its sanction in July 1908, and the bands were added to the towers in the summer of 1909.

With the speed of rural electrification, the Inspecting Committee recommended in 1953 that the lights be converted to electricity. Progress was slow, and overhead cables were not in the area until 1958. The dwellings were the first to be converted to electricity. Meanwhile, there had been a rethink regarding the lights, in so far as the Inspecting Committee, in 1957, decided to abandon the front and auxiliary lights, and replace the acetylene light in the rear tower with an electric light in a catadioptric lens, with a red sector over the dangerous Tuns Bank.

In 1979, automation led to the keeper being withdrawn and replaced by an attendant, Mr N. Smith. The attendant lives in the house nearest the lighthouse, and the other two dwellings were later converted to holiday homes for lighthouse staff and their families. The fog signal, still in use at this time, was replaced by an electric foghorn controlled by a fog detector. Consideration was given early in 1979 to making the station more compact by moving the cast-iron extension on the west tower to the east tower, but the Inspecting Committee, on tour in 1979, decided against this recommendation. ✳ *Fl (2) WRG 10s#*

Rathlin East

Rathlin Island can be found 5 miles off the Antrim coast. Prior to the Famine, this small, *L*-shaped island was home to more than a thousand people. With the failure of the potato crop, half of them left the island, never to return. These days, around a hundred people live on this historic island, many of them with roots on the island dating back hundreds of years. Several famous people have graced its shores, among them Robert the Bruce, who hid in one of the island's caves following defeat at Perth; it was at Rathlin that a spider is said to have inspired Bruce to his victory at the Battle of Bannockburn. Guglielmo Marconi also spent time on Rathlin, from where, in 1898, he conducted wireless trials.

Rathlin Island has three lighthouses, one at the east – the first to be built – another at the west and one at Rue Point. Application from mariners for a light on Rathlin Island was first made in 1827, but approval from Trinity House was not obtained until 1847, and construction did not commence until May 1849. The buildings were designed by Inspector George Halpin, and carried out by the Board's workmen.

Two lights – an upper occulting and lower fixed, so as not to be confused with other lights when approaching and passing through the North Channel – were established on 1 November 1856. The tower of the upper light is built of stone from the island, and stands 26.8 metres high. The light is 74 metres above high water, and originally had an occulting character of 50 seconds bright with 10 seconds dark. The light also showed over Carrick-a-Vaan Rock, off Kenbane Head on the mainland. The lower light consisted of a lantern placed close to the base of the tower. The light was 55.5 metres above high water and showed a fixed – or non-flashing – light.

The lower fixed light was discontinued on 1 July 1894, and at the same time the tower light was intensified. 1912 saw a further change to the main light: a completely new optic was installed with a vaporised-paraffin burner, giving four flashes every 20 seconds. The red sector over the Carrick-a-Vaan Rock was discontinued in 1938, and the light was converted to electricity in 1981. The colour of the tower seems to have been originally natural stone with a broad belt under the lantern balcony. The stone was painted white, though still with the red belt. This lasted for about 60 years, until 1933, when the red belt was changed to black, as it is today. ✷ *Fl (4) W 20s* ✷

Rathlin West

Rathlin West, which came into operation in 1919, is by far the most impressive of the island's lighthouses. It is unconventional in that, due to its elevated location and the need to ensure the light was not obscured by fog, the tower had to be built almost a third of the way down the cliff face. The lantern is located at the base of the tower, with the keepers' quarters overhead. It is a marvel of engineering, and one can only speculate at the difficulties involved in its establishment.

The first mention of a light on Rathlin West was made early in 1901, when a light was suggested either for Doone Point – on the east coast of the island, north of Rue Point – or at Rue Point itself. The proposed positions were probably too close to the already established light on Altacarry Head, but soon after the suggestion, the Board referred the subject to the Inspecting Committee. Differences of opinion were expressed by Trinity House and Irish Lights as to which headland – Bull Point or Crockantirrive – was the more suitable for the light and fog signal; one suggestion was to place the light on one and the fog signal on the other. During 1902, Trinity House visited the proposed sites on Rathlin, and experiments were carried out later to select the most suitable site for the fog signal. Crockantirrive was chosen, and the Board decided the name of the new station should be Rathlin West. Sanction was obtained from Trinity House for a light and siren-fog-signal station in 1903, and the Board of Trade gave its sanction in 1904.

Five years elapsed before the subject was brought up again, and the Board agreed to include the new light and fog signal in the 1910–11 estimates. Progress was slow, and during 1914, the Board of Trade enquired if the work could not be hastened. When consideration is given to the volume of concrete poured and set against the cliff at Crockantirrive, coupled with the inclined railway built at Corraghy for transporting materials, it is no wonder the building took so long. Towards the end of 1916, the light and dwellings were complete, and Captain Deane – the inspector – enquired if the Admiralty's views could be ascertained prior to issuing a Notice to Mariners for the new light. The Admiralty did not reply until early 1919, stating that it saw no reason why the light and fog signal should not be put into operation. A draft notice was subsequently approved by the Board for a light only, to be exhibited on 10 March 1919, with a character of one 0.4-second red flash every 5 seconds. The fog-signal Notice to Mariners was approved by the Board in October 1924, and established on 15 July 1925, with four 1.5-second blasts every 60 seconds. Rathlin West was converted from a manned paraffin light to unwatched electric light in 1983, and is monitored from Rathlin East. *Fl R 5s##

Rue Point

An unwatched light at Rue Point was recommended by the Inspecting Committee in July 1914 after a memorial, signed by master mariners, had been forwarded to the Commissioners from the Derry Chamber of Commerce. Sanction from Trinity House was obtained in November 1914, but the Board of Trade postponed the new light until 1916–17. Towards the end of 1915, the Board carried out the erection of a temporary white, double-flashing light for the Admiralty. It was established on 19 November 1915, without a Notice to Mariners being issued. The Board of Trade followed this up by stating that if the Admiralty was satisfied with the temporary light, it would not sanction a permanent structure.

In 1916, the Inspecting Committee recommended a permanent structure due to the high cost of running a temporary light, but the Board of Trade was not prepared to sanction during the war. An acetylene fog gun was also proposed by the Inspecting Committee, and with the Admiralty's blessing, this went into operation on 12 April 1917. A severe storm wrecked the temporary light in November 1917, so the light was transferred to the undamaged fog gun trestle. When the Admiralty suggested repositioning the light and fog signal on higher ground, the engineer –

Mr Scott – reported it was not practicable. The Board of Trade was approached again in 1918 with regard to a permanent structure, but replied that it could not sanction a new light out of present funds. It was not until 1920–21 that the six-sided concrete tower – still in existence – was constructed, with a water-to-carbine, acetylene generator housed inside, and with the light and fog-gun positioned on the roof.

Although two keepers were attached to Rue and living in the wooden hut when on duty, the reliability of the fog gun was never very satisfactory. Following a bad storm in January 1928, the Board of Trade enquired as to whether the gun could be made more reliable, and thus enable the keepers to be withdrawn. Efforts to do so were to no avail, and when the Inspecting Committee recommended discontinuing the fog signal, Trinity House and the Board agreed. The fog signal was withdrawn on 1 January 1931. The gun was overhauled and replaced the fog bell at Barr Point near Ferris Point at the entrance to Larne Lough.

Acetylene-generating plants, good and reliable as they were, do not last forever, and on 9 October 1965, Rue Point's light was converted to electricity, and is monitored from Rathlin East. In recent times, Rue Point – given its exposed location – was considered suitable for the siting of a wind charger, and this more economical source of power has proven quite successful there.

Like Tory, this is an isolated island which has avoided the hazards of tourism. I spent a lot of time on Rathlin, and a few years ago – when at the west lighthouse – I was invited to the first wedding on the island for many years. Naturally, this was quite an event, and lasted three days and nights; in fact, I do not remember a wedding like it. No trace of sectarianism ever rears its ugly head on Rathlin, and class and creed were united in one long festival. I might add that this particular feeling is not confined to weddings, and I know of no other island where peace and harmony reign so supreme, and neglect of one's fellow men is not tolerated. However, life is not idyllic here, as it can be on other islands, and being very northerly, it is one long struggle against the elements. The townland of Kebble, at the west of the island, is now designated as a nature reserve, and contains large colonies of breeding puffins, shearwaters and guillemots. There are also a few lakes on the island, which wild fowl frequent, thus enhancing the native's diet.

Rathlin is an old island, inhabited by prehistoric man 8,000 years ago. It would appear that the main industry then was the making and fashioning of tools made from the hard porcellanite stone found in the village of Brockley. Nowadays, the few natives that are left depend for a living on fishing, farming and the raising of cattle. Tourism is practically non-existent, as the only access to the island is by a long boat trip from Ballycastle. Incidentally, anyone who visits the island hoping to find the famed Bruce's Castle will be disappointed, as only a pile of rubble remains of that historic 'edifice'. ✷ *Fl (2) W 5s*

East Coast

Maidens

At the entrance to Larne Harbour, this low-lying, confined and utterly miserable rock had every right to be included in the list of 'hardship stations' which keepers had to endure years ago. It has been unwatched for some time, and is under the care of a shore attendant. The absence of human habitation has added greatly to its deterioration, and despite the best efforts of our maintenance staff, the place still reeks of a decay which is hard to define. I was on it one night in recent years and could not wait to get off.

I know an old principal keeper who used to down a couple of bottles of whiskey on the first day of his stints of duty there, and then retire to bed and let his assistants look after things. I never could determine what exactly was wrong with the Maidens – after all, it's just another rock in the sea. But I would rather spend a month on the Fastnet any time. There was a noticeable absence of tears from the lightkeepers when the light became automatic in 1977.

Maidens

In 1819, Inspector George Halpin visited the rocks, following application by Admiral Hallowell and the merchants of Larne for the establishment of a lighthouse on the Maidens rocks. The Inspector recommended two lighthouses, which were sanctioned by Trinity House in August 1924. The tower on the northern rock – known as the west tower – was 25 metres above high water, its light visible for 13 nautical miles. The tower on the southern rock – known as the east tower – was 29 metres high, its light visible for 14 nautical miles. The two towers – 780 metres apart – first exhibited lights on 5 January 1829.

In 1899, an auxiliary light was introduced to cover the Highland Rocks, and the light was built into a window of the east tower. In December 1898, the engineer – W. Douglass – proposed that a light-vessel with a powerful light and fog siren be moored north of the Highland Rocks, and that the west light be discontinued. On 12 March 1903, an improved light on the east tower was exhibited, and the west light discontinued. On 12 October 1977, the light was converted to electricity, and its range increased to 24 nautical miles. The station was made unwatched on 31 October 1977. ✹ *Fl (3) W 20s* *

Chaine Tower

The Irish round towers of the tenth, eleventh and twelfth centuries were not built as navigational lookouts or landmarks. They were usually attached to monastic settlements, and were invariably inland, well away from the coast. Their purpose, so we are told, was to provide a place of retreat during attacks or plundering raids on the settlement; hence, the only entrance was situated some considerable distance above the ground (with one exception, as far as I am aware – the tower on Scattery Island has a door at ground level).

Of the towers which might have proved useful navigational guides, one was on Scattery Island close to the entrance to the River Shannon, one was on Tory Island and another was to be found at Ardmore, County Waterford. At Killala, tucked up in a sheltered bay of the same name, west of Sligo, another round tower once proved itself of use to mariners. In 1819, the bishop of Killala pointed out to the Corporation that ships of over 5,000 tons using the port of Killala considered the round tower an invaluable landmark, but as it had recently been struck by lightning, it required repair. Inspector George Halpin visited the tower in 1823, and reported that, though it was badly cracked, the tower could be repaired in such a way as to preserve its appearance. The costs, he asserted, should be met from local harbour dues. The bishop was subsequently informed that, considering its position, it was not an object to which the Corporation's funds were applicable. It seems the tower remained in a state of disrepair for a further twenty years before another bishop had it repaired.

The Larne beacon – designed in the style of an early round tower – was built by public subscription and completed in January 1888. It received full approval from the Board of Trade and Commissioners of Irish Lights, and the Larne Harbour Authority undertook to maintain the tower. Inspector Boxer recommended that the beacon be painted black, but the Inspecting Committee disagreed, and the tower retained its natural stone colour. In April 1896, the Larne and Stranraer Steamship Joint Committee wrote to the Commissioners to draw their attention to the inadequate buoying of Hunter Rock off the entrance to Larne Harbour. The committee suggested that a light be fixed on the stone beacon (or round tower) on Sandy Bay Point. Two months later, the Inspecting Committee agreed to a light being placed in Chaine Tower, and suggested that the trustees of the tower be approached with a view to handing over the tower to the Commissioners. Later, the Inspecting

Committee stated that it was prepared to improve Larne Harbour (or Ferris Point) by raising it and placing two lights in Chaine Tower – one halfway down – as a guiding light for the passage between Hunter Rock and the shore. Mr D. MacDonald of Larne offered every facility to the Board's engineer, Mr W. Douglass, as he examined the tower with a view to converting it to a lighthouse. By the end of July, a letter had been received from the Chaine Memorial Trustees, stating that they had no objection to the Commissioners using the tower, provided that the exterior was not interfered with and the causeway maintained in proper order; in addition, it would be used solely as a lighthouse. The Commissioners agreed to the terms, and informed the trustees of the proposed alterations required to modify the tower. Mr MacDonald replied that there would be no objections to further openings in the tower so that a light could cover Hunter Rock.

Established on 1 July 1899, the new light gave a white and red flash every 5 seconds – that is, 3 seconds flash, 2 seconds dark. The power and range of the light, in the white and red sectors, were 1,000 and 300 candelas, and 10 and 7 nautical miles respectively. The tower is 28 metres high, and the light shines through a window 22 metres above high water. An additional assistant keeper for the Maidens lighthouse was sanctioned to keep watch at Chaine Tower, and early in 1900, a dwelling was rented in Larne for the keeper.

Conversion of the light from gas to electricity was approved in April 1930, but the changeover did not take place until 12 September 1935. Chaine Tower was the second light to be converted to electricity, Donaghadee – the first – having been converted a year earlier. The electric light at Chaine Tower gave an increased candle power in the white sector of 2,700. During April 1948, the DC supply was changed to AC. A further change took place on 19 June 1964 when the character was altered from occulting 5 seconds to isophase 5 seconds (i.e., 2.5-seconds flash, 2.5-seconds dark). A car-headlamp-type light now shines across the lough entrance to Ferris Point, indicating to the keeper on duty that the electricity supply is 'on'. If the supply fails, a 24-volt battery takes over automatically. ✳*Iso WR 5s*

Ferris Point

The light at Ferris Point was established on 1 February 1839, and at that time was known as Larne Lough lighthouse. The first request for a lighthouse to mark the entrance to Larne Harbour was made by the merchants of Larne in 1831. Sanction having been obtained, the plans for the lighthouse were completed by Inspector George Halpin in 1835. The building of the original slate-shingled, cut-stone tower was carried out between 1835 and 1838.

The original light was fixed, and consisted of a number of oil lamps in silvered-copper reflectors. A red sector was established over the Hunter Rocks at a later stage. The arrangement of oil lamps lasted until 1957, when conversion to electricity took place. A green sector was added to the light, and the character was changed from fixed to occulting every 2 seconds.

The old tower was replaced in 1976 during a modernisation plan which included the automation of the Maidens lighthouse and the provision of modern workshops for buoy maintenance. The Maidens shore dwellings, located in the Ferris Point compound, were also demolished. The lantern is now located on top of the tower and control rooms. The navigational light was upgraded from 250 to 1,000 watts on 27 May 1981. The character was also changed, to isophase 10 seconds. During the summer of 1983, the lantern from the old tower was refurbished, and is now sited at Carnlough Harbour as a tourist attraction.

The new concrete tower, with the lantern over the 'airport-style' watchtower, was ultra-modern in design, and contained every comfort for the lightkeepers. Although now sadly automated, the same facilities can be enjoyed by visiting maintenance personnel. It is a far cry from the 137-year-old slate-shingled stone tower which it replaced.

✳ *Iso WRG 10s*

Blackhead, Antrim

Heading south, we come to another particular favourite of mine – Blackhead in Antrim. There is another Blackhead, as we have seen, in County Clare, but the two Blackhead lighthouses are far enough apart so as not to cause confusion. It has always amused me that the local village for this lighthouse is actually called Whitehead. A charming little seaside resort – like so many that seem to abound on the Antrim coast – this one can be justly proud of its own yachting centre, quaint shops and spotless streets.

The lighthouse in Blackhead was first established in 1902, as indeed was the explosive fog signal. Nothing untoward seems to have happened at the lighthouse during the many years it was manned. In 1969, modernisation arrived, and the light was made electric. It remained manned until 1975. The explosive fog signal was discontinued in 1972 – as in all stations – primarily for security reasons.

I spent many happy days in Blackhead at this epitome of an unpretentious, well-maintained, headland lighthouse. For many years, it has been in the very capable hands of an attendant by the name of Johnny Connell, a former principal keeper on many of our major lighthouses, and a most hospitable man.

When in Blackhead, I used to take every opportunity to visit Belfast so as to see avant-garde films that because of censorship could not be shown in Dublin. The cinema excepted, the Belfast nightlife was very dull, even during those relatively calm days before the Troubles. The city was like a morgue after 10.30 p.m., and it was difficult to get so much as a cup of coffee after the pictures. Compare that with Dublin in the same era, when things were only beginning to get into top gear at such an early hour! ✳ *Fl W 3s*

Mew Island

The present lighthouse and fog signal on Mew Island was established on 1 November 1884, when its predecessor on Lighthouse Island (or Lesser Copeland Island) was discontinued. The latter was established in the early eighteenth century, being one of four cottage-type, coal-burning lights around the Irish coast, the others being at Loophead, the Old Head of Kinsale and Howth Head. A fifth coal-burning light was exhibited on top of Hook Tower. Prior to Copeland, there had been a light at Island Magee near Carrickfergus – probably another cottage-type light. This was during the 1660s, and it lasted only three to four years. In 1796, Thomas Rogers added a 6-foot-diameter lantern to a corner on top of the Copeland Island 12-metre-high square tower, and changed the lighting from coal to oil, using six Argand lamps, each with its own reflector. After the Revenue Commissioners handed over the light-house in 1810 to the Corporation for Preserving and Improving the Port of Dublin, one of the first stations to be improved was Copeland. A 52-foot-high tower and lantern were constructed alongside the old tower to Mr George Halpin's design, and a fixed light with 27 Argand lamps and reflectors was lit on 24 January 1815. The actual light was 39 metres above sea level.

Early in 1851, a large fog bell operated by a weight-driven machine periodically wound up by the keepers was located in the old lighthouse tower. As commerce increased and sailing vessels were being replaced by steam-driven vessels, a better-positioned light was sought. In January 1875, the Belfast Harbour Commissioners was the first to request the removal of the Copeland light to Mew Island. Work on the new station eventually commenced in 1882. Designed by Mr W. Douglass, chief engineer to the Irish Lights Commissioners, the new light and character of four 4-second flashes in 20 seconds was repeated every minute. With a total of 324 jets, the candle power increased from 13,500 to 189,500.

In 1928, the gas-making plant – the last on the coast – was discontinued, and the ex-Tory Island biform (two-tier) optic replaced the original triform, which had been giving trouble for some time. Paraffin-vapour burners were used instead of coal burners, and the character was altered to four flashes every half minute. Paraffin gave way to electric

Mew Island

lamps on 15 July 1969. A radio beacon was established on 8 August 1949, and the tower, which had always been painted black, acquired a 27-foot-deep white band halfway up in January 1954.

The keepers' shore dwellings at Donaghadee were sold in October 1967, and the keepers then lived in their own homes, travelling to and from Donaghadee when their tour of duty on the island commenced or finished. A local boat contractor carried out reliefs from Donaghadee every two weeks. In July 1981, the station was automated.

For many years, Mew Island had been referred to in the service as the 'gentleman's station'. How it acquired this envious title no one seems to know. Be that as it may, over the years, the station has been manned by our more moderate and benign lightkeepers, and there has always been a remarkable air of tranquillity between the incumbents on the island and the visitors who land on it. One thing I regret is the demise of a super little pitch-and-putt course that afforded me immense pleasure when I was there, and which generated intense rivalry between depot personnel and the lightkeepers. Successive keepers, however, have different priorities, and – like the goats on the Tearaght that were allowed to go wild after being domesticated for many years – some keepers on Mew had neither the time nor the inclination to keep that little golf course functional. ✴ *Fl (4) W 30s##*

Donaghadee

This pleasant County Down seaside resort developed when the 'short sea route' – a distance of around 35 kilometres – to Portpatrick in Wigtownshire was established in 1662, and which was to operate for 200 years. Unfortunately, the route declined, mainly due to the lack of immediate railway facilities, and because as vessels became larger the difficult access into Portpatrick and shelter at Donaghadee was virtually impossible in easterly winds. In spite of the Belfast and County Down railway reaching Donaghadee in 1861, and the railway to Portpatrick the following year, attention was drawn to a new route between Larne and Stranraer, which eventually took over in 1871. An earlier attempt at establishing this route had been made in 1862; the route then lasted just over a year.

With the advent of steam-driven paddle vessels – the first to be used on the Donaghadee route was in 1825 – the Post Office improved the harbour facilities at both Donaghadee and Portpatrick, contributing a large sum of money towards their construction. Designed by John Rennie, the project was completed by his son, Sir John Rennie. Both were eminent civil engineers of their time.

The light was established in 1836 with a fixed character, showing red mainly to seaward and white over the harbour and towards Belfast Lough. The tower is built of cut limestone, fluted, and in its early days retained its natural grey colour. A decision was taken some time between 1869 and 1875 to paint the tower, lantern and dome white, with a black plinth. This is how the lighthouse appears today.

A dwelling was suggested for the keeper in 1841, and land near the foot of the pier was rented from the Board of Works. The ground, however, became a yard for maintenance for local Donaghadee buoys, and the dwelling was not built until 1864. The keeper, in the meantime, continued to live in a house in the town, rented by the Ballast Board.

A serious fire damaged the optic and lantern on 12 May 1900, and a temporary light had to be shown while a new optic was obtained and the damaged lantern repaired. This was completed by September of the same year. Conversion to unwatched electric was on 2 October 1934, Donaghadee thus having the distinction of being the first Irish lighthouse to be converted to electricity. Chaine Tower at Larne followed the next year, and Tuskar in 1938. The character of the new electric light was isophase, white every 4 seconds, and the red sector was discontinued. The power was considerably increased, from less than 1,000 to 20,000 candelas. In 1967, an automatic standby to a mains generator was installed in the base of the tower, a red sector was re-established, and a new lamp changer with two electric lamps was fitted into the optic. These alterations took place in conjunction with the withdrawal of the *Skulmartin* light vessel and the establishment of a high-focal-plane buoy in its stead. ✳*Iso WR 4s*

Angus Rock

It is pleasing to report the establishment of a new light on an old beacon that had remained dark since its construction. The beacon marks the existence of a rock, the position of which has been extremely hazardous for years to shipping using Strangford Lough.

A beacon was erected as far back as 1715, but an inadvertently fired shell from a Revenue boat, *Revenge* – in 1797 – partly demolished it. Over the years, numerous requests to place a light on Angus went unheeded, even though it was reported that over 70 boats had been either lost or damaged in the area from 1833–47. As Belfast Lough prospered, Strangford declined, and it was only the perseverance of the Strangford traders that caused a new granite beacon to be built between 1850–54. This had provision for a light at a future date.

Incredibly, it was not until 7 April 1983 that a light finally appeared on this beacon that had remained dark for so many years. In honour of this auspicious occasion, the Reverend W.E. Kennedy of Strangford was prompted to put pen to paper and write this poem (I am grateful for permission to include it here):

For many years I've stood like silent ghost upon the Angus Rock
I've braved the storm, the angry sea, I've heard the sailors mock
'What right have you,' must they not say, 'to call yourself a light?'
When fog abounds and dark comes down you vanish in the night.
I know I am a fraud, a sham, no use to man or beast
But what is this? Good news I hear: that after all these years
A light will flash from out my head, an end to all my tears
No more shall passing sailors sneer or lightless lighthouse mock
For red-hued light will guide them home, the flash of Angus Rock.

Nearby, the South Rock light-ship does duty. It's interesting to note that a lighthouse once marked the South Rock, and was known in its early days as the Kilwarlin lighthouse, after Lord Kilwarlin, Marquis of Downshire, one of its promoters. Designed by Thomas Rogers, it was established on 25 March 1797, and had the distinction of being the first wave-washed, rock lighthouse around the Irish coast. Of the thirteen lighthouses at the time, it was the only one with a revolving optic. A bell was sounded during foggy weather conditions.

In 1874, Trinity House decided to replace the lighthouse with a light-vessel, and in April 1877, the assistant inspector reported that a light-vessel had been placed off the South Rock by the service steamer, *Alert*. The light character of the light-vessel was the same as that at the light-house, but the fog signal was changed from a bell to a gun, and fired once every 15 minutes in fog. On the same day that the light-vessel was put into service, the South Rock lighthouse was discontinued and became an unlighted beacon.

Although no light now shines from Kilwarlin, a recent inspection revealed it to be in a remarkable state of preservation, considering it has been uninhabited for over 100 years – a tribute, no doubt, to its designer and builder, Thomas Rogers. ✳*Fl R 5s*

St John's Point – close to the village of Kilough – is another of lighthouse which, though unsung and unseen, is still worth a visit. The playwright and wit, Brendan Behan, made his mark at St John's lighthouse way back in 1950 when still employed by Irish Lights as a painter; I happened to meet him during that period. His work, it seems, was not appreciated by the principal keeper at St John's, a Mr D. Blakely. In a scathing letter to headquarters, Behan was castigated for all manner of shortcomings:

> Sir, I have to report the painter B. Behan absent from his work all day yesterday and not returning to station until 1.25 a.m. this morning. No work has been carried out by him yesterday (Tuesday). I also have to report that his attitude here is one of careless indifference and no respect for Commissioners property or stores. He is wilfully wasting materials, opening drums and paint tins by blows from a heavy hammer, spilling the contents which is now running out of the paint store door. Drums of water-wash opened and exposed to the weather – no cleaning up of any mess but he tramps through everything. His language is filthy and he is not amenable to any law or order.
>
> He has ruined the wall surface of one wall in No.1 Dwelling by burning. He mixes

putty, paint, etc. with his bare hands and wipes off nothing. The spare house which was clean and ready for painters has been turned into a filthy shambles inside a week. Empty stinking milk bottles, articles of food, coal, ashes and other debris litter the floor of the place which is now in a scandalous condition of dirt.

I invite any official of the Irish Lights to inspect this station and verify these statements.

He is the worst specimen I have met in 30 years service. I urge his dismissal from the job now before good material is rendered useless and the place ruined.

Your obedient Servant,
D. Blakely Principal Keeper

The light, at 18.9 metres above high water, was established on 1 May 1844, with an intermittent, or occulting, character: 45-second flash, 15 seconds dark. The light was changed from white to red on 1 July 1860. On 27 May 1875, the

St John's Point, Down

light source was converted from oil to coal gas, supplied from a gas plant at the station.

A recommendation to improve the marking of the County Down coast resulted in the tower being raised – the light was now 36.5 metres above high water – and the establishment of a fog signal – with a character blast of 2 seconds every 60 seconds – and an auxiliary light over Dundrum Bay. In 1902, the white tower was given the addition of three black bands.

With the introduction of a biform lens and the replacement of the gas jets with incandescent vaporised-paraffin burners, the main light was improved in March 1909. The colour also changed from red to white, and the character of the new light to group flash (two) every 7.5 seconds. The auxiliary light was converted to a paraffin-vapour burner on 18 October 1910. A further alteration was made to the colour scheme in 1954, when the tower was painted black with two yellow bands. *Q (2) W 7.5s#*

Carlingford

Irish Lights maintains four lights in the Carlingford area – two leading lights, Haulbowline in the middle of the lough, and Greenore – a harbour light on Greenore Point. We shall deal firstly with the leading lights.

Early in 1868, the Carlingford Lough Commissioners informed the Irish Lights Commissioners that they were deepening the channel through the bar into Carlingford Lough, and desired to erect leading lights for the channel. The Inspecting Committee visited Carlingford Lough, and in its report recommended that the two lights be erected. By July 1868, it had been agreed that the lights should come under the Mercantile Marine Fund, and the Carlingford Commissioners requested Irish Lights to make arrangements for the construction of the two lights.

The lights are screw-pile, latticed-steel structures, with a small housing for the light on top. Situated 457 metres apart, the rear structure – Green Island – is 13.7 metres above high water, while the front structure – Vidal Bank – is 8.8 metres high. Fixed, white lights were established on 28 February 1873, and the structures were painted red with a white housing for the light, which at that time was an oil lamp.

In 1922, the lights were converted to unwatched acetylene with a water-to-carbide generator. The character of the lights was fixed to occulting, giving a 2-second flash every 3 seconds. In 1967, propane cylinders replaced the acetylene generators, and the light source was changed to a mantle from a fantail flame. To comply with regulations issued in the 1970s, the colour of the structures was changed from red to green. ✸ *Front: Oc W 3s · Rear: Oc W 3s*

Haulbowline

I believe I have the dubious distinction of having spent the longest single period at this lighthouse (though the builders may have exceeded my tenure there). The only accommodation is in the towers, and the concrete landing at the bottom – on the outside of the tower – is no more than ten or fifteen paces. Lighthouses were ordinarily relieved every fortnight, but this rock was so bad it had a boat twice a week, on Tuesdays and Fridays. The keepers' period of duty alternated between one and two weeks. Through an error in communication and due to a belief that I had to stay on the lighthouse until my job of work was complete, I spent six of the most confined weeks of my life practically locked up in that tower.

On the sixth Sunday morning – which was good for a change – I was down early on the landing and hailed a passing boat, owned by Willie John Cunningham. Willie John was out hauling his lobster pots, but he was also the boat contractor for the lighthouse. He lived at the head of the pier in a place called Greencastle – on the northern side of the lough – and governed practically everything that moved on the water all the way up to Newry. Willie John did everything: he was the pilot, a fisherman, had his own strawberry beds, carried out the reliefs, and maintained all the harbour buoys as well. I never knew a man to pack so much into a day. But to return to my 'day off': intending to go ashore for a few hours, I was dressed in just a shirt and pants. I hitched a lift into Kilkeel, about 5 miles away, and went into the Royal Hotel. There, I ordered a few drinks, was put into a room by myself with all the Sunday papers, and the door was locked – a precaution, I was told, as drink was not supposed to be served in the North on Sundays in those days. Every so often, the owner looked in to see how things were going, and then another round was ordered. Lunch and tea followed, by which time I was in no mood to return to my 'prison'. Having heard talk of a bus taking a crowd to a dance somewhere up in the mountains, I hopped aboard. The dance lasted until the early hours of the morning, and by that time I had managed to make 'contact', and after the bus landed us back in Kilkeel, I walked her the 3 miles to a farmhouse. I was still in shirt and pants and it was now very cold. A handy outhouse came to our rescue, and afterwards she was good enough to loan me a bike to get back to Greencastle, 8 miles away. I pulled up at the pier at nine-thirty that morning, just as Willie John was casting off his boat. The principal keeper reported me for my transgression, but got a reprimand himself for not informing me of my shore-leave rights. Willie John is dead since, but his sons carry on the tradition of their father in maintaining the lights in the lough.

At such a confined tower as Haulbowline, living was both crude and unorthodox. Lack of water was a constant problem as there was no catchment area, and water had to be carried out by the contractor's boat every day. One basin of water each day was our daily ration, which was not nearly sufficient. Nevertheless, there was one particular keeper who managed, by some adroit means, to always appear immaculately turned out – an achievement that caused much speculation and envy among his fellow keepers.

Haulbowline – or Carlingford Bar, as it is sometimes called – is a main sea light and also serves to guide vessels through the entrance channel into Carlingford Lough. The lighthouse was built in 1817 at the behest of the merchants of Newry, as a replacement for the 1803 Cranfield Point lighthouse. The merchants were concerned about the suitability of the old lighthouse for marking the dangerous rocks at the entrance to Carlingford Lough, and also because of its inadequacy as a guide for vessels at the west end of the Lough.

Haulbowline

The cut-stone tower was designed by Mr George Halpin, and built under his direction by workmen of the Board. Its overall height is 34 metres, and the main light is 32 metres above high water. The tower was painted white, and remained so until 1946, when it was changed to its natural stone colour. The fixed white light was also exhibited from a small lantern approximately halfway up the seaward side of the tower. During daytime, a large ball was hoisted on a mast above the lantern to indicate the tide. A bell was struck by a machine every half-minute during foggy weather. On 1 September 1898, the fog bell was changed to an explosive fog signal, giving one report every 10 minutes. This was changed to every 5 minutes in 1932. In 1965, when the light was made unwatched, a sound-emitter with a character of one blast every 30 seconds replaced the explosive signal.

From 1824 to 1922, the keepers and their families lived in the Cranfield Point lighthouse dwellings. New dwellings were built at Greenore in 1922, and subsequently sold after the light became unwatched. Cranfield Point lighthouse tower became a victim of coastal erosion, and in the early 1860s, tumbled onto what had become the foreshore. ✱ *Fl (3) W 10s#*

Dundalk

This busy industrial cross-border town has its mythical and historical roots dating back to Cúchulainn, Delga (whose fort the town is named after), Queen Maeve, the Norsemen, Normans, Jacobites and Williamites; even Agnes, the eldest sister of Scotland's Robert Burns, is buried in St Nicholas' churchyard.

On 13 January 1846, the Dundalk Harbour Commissioners wrote to the Corporation requesting it consider two suitable lighthouses to guide the ever-increasing number of vessels into the harbour. Inspector George Halpin reported favourably on the issue, though he recognised the difficulty in marking the channel. Two further approaches were made to the Board – once again by the Harbour Commissioners, and also by Daniel O'Connell, the Member of Parliament for Dundalk. The outcome was a recommendation by Inspector Halpin for a Mitchell's patent screw-pile structure, utilising the wrought and cast-iron screw pile patented by Alexander Mitchell, a blind Belfast engineer. Mitchell's screw-pile principle was also applied to piers, beacons and moorings. In the case of a lighthouse, the piles – screwed into the sand – support a wooden decking upon which is placed accommodation and a small lantern. Mitchell's design was also adopted at Hollywood Bank in Belfast Lough (1848) – destroyed by a collision in March 1889 – Spit Bank at Cobh (1853), and Dundalk (1855). Unsuccessful attempts to place screw piles were made on the Kish, Arklow and Backwater Banks.

The light on Dundalk was eventually established on the night of 18 June 1855; its cost by the close of that year was £6,769. The structure – painted white with red piles – was now on the north bank of the channel. The light, 10 metres above high water, was a fourth-order dioptric, flashing white, with red sectors every 15 seconds. The optic was revolved by a weight-driven machine. Soon after the light was established, Inspector Halpin recommended a fog-signal bell, and this came into operation in November 1860, paid for by the Harbour Commissioners. The bell was struck six times every minute by another weight-driven machine, wound up by the keeper on duty. Dundalk's tides make it difficult to land on the lighthouse at certain times, as the area around the base dries out.

The Inspecting Committee on tour in 1962 recommended that Dundalk pile light be converted to electricity and made unwatched, but this was postponed for a few years. The conversion got underway in early 1967, and the electric light – of 187,000 candelas – was first exhibited on 17 December 1968. A foghorn with a diaphone was activated in 1969, and the light and foghorn are now monitored ashore by an attendant. The old fog-signal bell – being the property of the Harbour Commissioners – was returned to its owners.

I was in at the death of Dundalk lighthouse as a manned structure, and it was a depressing scene. The last principal keeper on Dundalk was Ambrose (Ambi) Butler, and I witnessed him crying bitterly one day during the demolition of his beloved abode. He used to recount the many years in his lighthouse, and how it was possible to slip ashore to Giles Quay for a few pints when the tide was out, and the frantic efforts to beat the tide on the way back. There was a boat for emergencies, but as far as I know, only one man ever availed of this asset: my friend, Bill Hamilton, whom we met at Hook Head. Ambi also recounted the near misses by big boats during foggy periods, and the way gales and tremendous seas shook his 'lighthouse on stilts', as he used to call it. Despite these hazards, it was obvious he missed his routine of years and the important part he played in the nautical life of Dundalk Bay. Now witnessing the demise of a lifestyle, it was no wonder he was sad. Automation – inevitable and necessary though it be – has a lot to answer for. *Fl WR 15s#

Rockabill

When Rockabill was established on 1 July 1860, the old lighthouse at Balbriggan was demoted to minor harbour light, and is no longer in the care of Irish Lights. When Balbriggan light underwent final changes in October 1960, it was decided to house it in two superimposed lenses, one in use and the other as a standby on top of the tower. The existing lantern had to be removed for this operation; from an aesthetic point of view it did not improve the appearance of the tower, and it now looks as if it had been decapitated at some time. Incidentally, just beyond the harbour lies a perch called Taylor Rock Perch, and I used to find difficulty in convincing the new incumbents to the service that this name was sheer coincidence and had nothing at all to do with me for services rendered. I am so grateful to have proven more durable (to date anyway!) than my illustrious namesake, because despite our best endeavours, it is continually being washed away.

To return to Rockabill, the tower was built on the summit of the larger and more southerly of the two rocks named Rockabill at the behest of the Drogheda Harbour Commissioners. Making their submission in October 1837, the Commissioners asserted that the shipping which frequented Drogheda would cheerfully pay a toll towards a light on Rockabill. The Ballast Board concurred, but insisted the toll should be no more than that charged for the light at Balbriggan. Trinity House declined to give sanction, and the project remained in abeyance until August 1853, when the Committee of Inspection, accompanied by the deputy master, Captain Sheppard, and five 'elder brethren', appeared to favour the project. It was brought before the Board in September, and was sanctioned in November, though the Ballast Board had great difficulty discovering to whom the rock belonged and in obtaining ownership. Nevertheless, George Halpin, chief engineer, prepared plans in 1855 and advertised for tenders; the contract went to Mr Burgess of Limerick. The granite for the tower and dwellings came from the Mourne Mountains, the limestone from Skerries and the rubble from Rockabill. The light is 42 metres above high water. The total cost of the buildings, tower, walls and apparatus was £13,248. A report to the Board from George Halpin, dated 5 July 1860, stated that at sunset on 1 July, the Rockabill light was exhibited punctually, and that its brilliance surpassed any other catoptric light on the east coast.

In 1872, a gas-producing plant was installed, and continued in use until 1905 when the light was converted to paraffin. This source of power was utilised until 1975, when the light was converted to electricity. Automation naturally negated the need for the lightkeepers' shore dwellings in Skerries, and so were sold.

I remember Rockabill for two reasons. Firstly, because it is frustratingly near that lovely seaside town of Skerries. Secondly, because it was almost destroyed by fire in 1973. By 'frustratingly' near Skerries, I mean it is so close that the sounds and – at times – the smells of that town are so near that one never actually settles down in the station. I have always contended that if one had to be out on a rock lighthouse, let it be one where no distractions are allowed to interfere with the solitude. As there is absolutely nothing anyone can do about the isolation, I would always opt for places such as the Fastnet or Tearaght, in preference to Rockabill. For much the same reason, I disliked Skerries in the summertime, when hordes of visitors arrived, some of whom asked the most appallingly banal questions and looked on us as virtual freaks. Lightkeepers are human, and to prove it, I will recount an incident related to me by an ex-principal keeper of Rockabill. Apparently, his turn of duty entitled him to spend Christmas at home with his family for the first time in many years, and he was ecstatic at the prospect. But a few days before the relief on 23 December, his assistant ashore – a great friend of his who lived beside him in the quarters – declared sick. So the principal keeper was doomed to spend yet another Christmas away from home. Imagine his feelings when, looking through his telescope on Christmas morning, he saw his 'sick' friend making his way to the church in Skerries. Needless to say, relations remained strained ever after.

The fire at Rockabill occurred in the lantern on 13 June 1973, and caused considerable damage. During investigations, it was found that a crack in the protective curtain around the lantern had allowed the sun's rays to penetrate and make contact with the powerful 'bullseye' of the lens. Timber frames, perspex glass and most of the lantern glass were destroyed. A temporary light was arranged, and for the first night ever, a white light shone ashore in Skerries, causing much discussion and speculation. It remained like that until replacement frames and ruby glass were refitted in the lantern. As a result of the fire, instructions were issued for all lenses to be rotated slowly as a fire-prevention measure.

Such mishaps are rare, and great credit is due to all involved for maintaining a fine record of service on the coast. *Fl WR 12s#

Baily

Looking out over Dublin Bay, one cannot but notice at least four lighthouses – the Baily in Howth, the East and West piers in Dún Laoghaire, and the comparatively new Kish far out into the bay. There is a fifth – the Muglins – but on the south side one has to get near Dalkey before this becomes visible from the land. The Baily deserves pride of place on our itinerary, as this is where all light-keepers got their preliminary schooling before being sent out on the coast. Here, the keeper received training in the most modern

Baily

methods of communication and general lighthouse duties. After a period as a supernumerary assistant keeper on many stations around the coast – doing relief duty for keepers who might be ill or on leave – he would be appointed to a specific station and remained there for anything up to four years. As he progressed from station to station, he would gradually rise to the rank of principal keeper and, after periods spent on various rock stations, would most probably be allotted a shore station. The normal retiring age was 60 years, but he could still play an active part in the service if he opted for one of the many unwatched lights where vacancies existed. Should that event occur, it could truly be said he had dedicated his adult life to the service of the 'Lights'.

In 1655, Sir Robert Reading was granted letters patent by King Charles II to build six lighthouses around the coast of Ireland: one at Kinsale, one at Barry Óg's castle in Kinsale (at what is now called Charlesfort), a third at Hook Tower, the fourth at the Isle of Magee (near Carrickfergus), and two at Howth – one 'mark to land', the other 'to come over the bar'. The latter was short-lived and was replaced by a perch and buoy close to the bar in Dublin Bay. The surviving lighthouse at Howth – the Baily – is a cottage-type lighthouse. Established around 1667, it consisted of a small cottage with a coal-burning beacon atop a square tower positioned against the cottage's eastern gable wall. Coal and other necessities were brought up by horses, carts and carriages from the quay specially built for the lighthouse at the village of Howth.

In 1790, Thomas Rogers – lighthouse contractor and inspector for the Revenue Commissioners – replaced the coal-burning light with a tower and lantern. The light source was six Argand oil lamps, each with a silvered-copper parabolic reflector to direct the light through six 'bulls-eye' panes – acting as crude lenses – set in the lantern. In common with a number of its contemporaries, the light was often obscured by mist or cloud due to its position high on the hill. In December 1811, the

Corporation for Preserving and Improving the Port of Dublin, which had taken over the fourteen coastal lighthouses from the Revenue Commissioners in 1810, sought to remedy this visibility problem by recommending the light be repositioned lower down on the headland at the Little Baily or Duncriffan where, almost 2,000 years earlier, King Crimthan had his fortress headquarters. The new tower and keeper's dwelling were designed by George Halpin, who also supervised the construction carried out by the Board's tradesmen.

The fixed, white, catoptric light, comprising 24 Argand oil lamps and reflectors, was established on 17 March 1814, 41 metres above high water. The cut-granite tower was painted white, and remained so until 1910 when, on the recommendation of the chief engineer, it reverted to its natural granite colour.

Over the years, a number of vessels have run up against the rocks or cliffs around Howth Head. One such mishap occurred on 3 August 1846, when the City of Dublin Steam Packet Company's paddle steamer, *Prince*, struck the cliffs in thick fog near the Nose of Howth, 2.5 kilometres north of the Baily. The Board could not be sure if fog bells would have prevented the accident, but felt it would be advisable to erect bells sounded by machinery at the station.

Almost seven years later – during the night of 15 February 1853 – another City of Dublin Steam Packet Company vessel came to grief at Howth. The PS (Paddle Steamer) *Queen Victoria* – approaching Dublin from Liverpool – ran onto the Casana Rock between the Nose and the Baily during a snowstorm. Eight of the passengers jumped ashore and made their way up the cliff to the Baily lighthouse. The captain managed to reverse the vessel off the rocks, but severe damage caused it to fill with water. The ship drifted towards the Baily, struck the rocks below the lighthouse and sank with her bowsprit touching the shore. Another City of Dublin Steam Packet Company vessel, the PS *Roscommon*, went to the rescue of the passengers still on board, saving between 40 and 50. Unfortunately, around 60 were drowned, among them the captain.

A protracted trial found the captain and mate guilty of culpable negligence in failing to reduce speed during a snowstorm, which had obscured the lights on land. The Board's own inquiry found that when the *Queen Victoria* struck the cliff below the lighthouse, the assistant keeper – who should have been on watch – was, in fact, in bed. Needless to say, the man was dismissed from the service.

The recommendation for fog bells at the Baily had been made in 1846 – seven years prior to the *Queen Victoria* tragedy. George Halpin explained that the urgency of other works being undertaken around the coast caused the erection of the bell at the Baily to be postponed. Two months after the loss of the *Queen Victoria*, the Corporation informed the Board of Trade that the fog bell was in the course of erection. Operating by the end of April 1853, the fog bell was replaced in 1879 by an air-trumpet-sounding horn which, in turn, was replaced by a siren in 1879.

Around 1865, Mr John R. Wigham, of Messrs Edmundson and Company, patented his inventions for illuminating lighthouses with gas, and that same year, the Board directed Mr Wigham to commence experiments at the Baily. At first, the gas was made from oil in the gasworks at the station, then shale, and finally rich channel coal. In the wake of this success, nine other stations were converted to either oil or coal gas.

During 1897, Mr W. Douglass, the chief engineer, recommended that the Baily light be improved and converted to flashing. Chance Brothers of Birmingham supplied the first-order optic, a pedestal with mercury float and a rotation machine; coal gas was retained as the light source. The new light came into operation on 1 January 1902, with a character of one flash every 30 seconds. Along with many other conversions to incandescent vaporised paraffin around the coast, the Baily's gas light source was changed in October 1908. Today, the Baily light is electric, has a light intensity of almost 1 million candle power and a range of 26 nautical miles. The 1902 optic, pedestal and rotation machine are preserved in the Maritime Institute of Ireland's Museum at Dún Laoghaire.

Two semi-detached dwellings for assistant keepers were built on the hill to the north of the lighthouse in 1892, and a very fine, detached, two-storey house was built for the principal keeper in 1953 in the yard below the lighthouse. What became known as the 'Baily Hilton' was constructed in 1973 below the lighthouse on the opposite side of the yard to the principal keeper's dwelling. This excellent modern accommodation was for the supernumerary assistant keepers. In 1993, the Baily became the landward base for helicopter reliefs to Kish and Rockabill lighthouses.

Among the many incidents to have been witnessed at the Baily, a particularly spectacular one occurred at noon on 11 September 1910, when the principal keeper, J. Watson, observed a biplane approaching the station from the east. The aircraft circled and dropped into the sea just 90 metres from the Dublin side of the Baily. The aviator swam towards the rocks, and Mr Watson helped him ashore. The pilot was Mr Robert Lorraine, and he had flown his aircraft from Holyhead. The *Adelia* – a steamer belonging to coal merchants Tedcastle's – passed the scene shortly afterwards, and the captain's attention was drawn to the machine in the water. A boat was lowered, the biplane was taken in tow, brought alongside the ship and hoisted on board. Mr Lorraine requested that the principal keeper put him on board the *Adelia* so that he could look after his machine – a request Mr Watson was able to fulfil by utilising a boat kept at the station for use by tradesmen. When the adroit Mr Watson attempted to telephone the coastguards and the GPO, he found the wire was broken. This he successfully repaired, and was able then to report the aircraft incident to the authorities. Quite an astute lightkeeper, our Mr Watson! ✳*Fl W 15s*##

Howth

The light at Howth was established by Sir Robert Reading. As mentioned earlier, his letter-patent permitted him to establish lights at various points around the country, including 'the hill of Howth', though Parliament would take another six years before granting specific permission for the construction of a light at Howth, which came into service in 1671. The granting of a lighthouse franchise to Sir Robert in 1665 probably had something to do with his being a member of the Irish Parliament; some things never change! Naturally, he was authorised to levy dues from shipping, which, according to parliamentary records, amounted to 'one penny per ton on all inward and outward bound ships; boats; crayers and ketches', while foreign ships were obliged to stump up 'a charge of two pence per ton'. Fishing vessels operating from any Irish port were also hit with a bill: 'they shall pay only ten shillings a year, each at the respective seasons of fishing'. The French did not get off lightly, either. According to Sir Robert's patent, 'all ships belonging to the subjects of the King of France and trading to or sailing by any harbour in Ireland, shall pay the same due per ton coming in or out, as is charged upon our ships trading to Bordeaux in France, towards the maintenance of the lighthouse of Cordouan, but such duty shall not be less than two pence per ton.' Sad to report for Sir Robert that the project failed, primarily due to the failure of many shipowners and masters to make payments. Sir Robert, of course, had most of the money spent before it was actually earned, and was obliged to surrender his interest in lighthouses in order to stay out of the debtors' prison.

Howth is one of the few harbour lights under the authority of Irish Lights, the majority being in the capable hands of the various harbour boards. I had the pleasure of knowing some of the previous occupants very well. A particularly charming couple were Mr and Mrs John Boyle.

John had been, of all things, a policeman prior to being appointed attendant at Howth. A man with a boundless love of the sea, he had applied for the position when it became vacant and, to his amazement and delight, got the job. He kept a boat in the harbour where he and his family spent many years. Mrs Boyle was well known in the Irish music business. She and John would drive up the pier in a battered old car, leave it at the entrance gate and get the bus into Monkstown, where Mrs Boyle regularly performed in the Comhaltas Ceoltoirí Éireann premises. Tragedy befell them when their son, who had sailed single-handed across the Atlantic, died suddenly while still young. John himself opened the door of his lighthouse one morning, took a few steps outside and died there on his beloved pier. He would not have wished for a happier end.

✷ *Fl (2) WR 7.5s*

Dún Laoghaire East and West

Dún Laoghaire East and West pier lighthouses are familiar to most Dubliners and to all those emigrants who have used the mail boat. Before the current structures were built, temporary lights were established on the east pier in 1822, and on the west in 1841. George Halpin designed these granite lighthouses, and supervised construction. The East light was completed first, in 1841, with the West light being displayed in 1850. Both were converted to electricity in 1968, and are now unmanned.

In 1996, the lanterns of the East and West lighthouses were painted red and green respectively – nautical characteristics to facilitate the new high-speed ferry using Dún Laoghaire Harbour. The character of the East light was changed to two red flash every 10 seconds with an intensity of 225,000 candelas and a range of 17 nautical miles, whilst the West light flashes green. ✷*East: Fl (2) R 10s · West: Fl (2) G 7.5s#*

Kish

The Kish Bank lighthouse was built in 1965 as a replacement for the light-ship that had serviced this area since 1811. Kish lighthouse is a unique structure in that a new concept of design enabled the tower to be telescoped when in position on its station. Built in Dún Laoghaire Harbour, it kept many people intrigued during construction. When the first base cracked, heads were seen to shake, but work progressed, and today the Kish is one of the most modern – and perhaps the most beautiful – of lighthouses on our coast. Incidentally, the first base was towed out to Greystones and now forms part of its harbour structure. A feature of the Kish is the helicopter pad which forms the roof and from where the reliefs for keepers were ferried to and fro. This lighthouse was considered to be of such importance that it was equipped with a unique system for intensifying the light during fog from its normal 2 million candelas to 3 million. This was the only lighthouse on the coast with such a feature. The tower is almost 30 metres, and the beam can be seen for 22 nautical miles.

The range of navigational aids is very impressive, and includes an electric foghorn with a range of 3.9 nautical miles, with two blasts every 30 seconds. Electric cranes do all the manual work, and fire fighting is provided on all floors. Smoke detectors are everywhere.

I have been on the Kish many times and, compared to most stations, the quarters are ultra modern, with a well-equipped kitchen, a separate dining room, a television lounge and a hobbies room, which added enormously to the keepers' comforts. If I had any fault to find with the Kish, it was that I found it unbearably hot at times. Indeed, on one of my stays there, the combination of heat and the fact that nearly all movement is either up or down stairs caused me to lose quite an amount of weight. On reflection, however, I think I could do with another visit there shortly.

The Kish was automated in April 1992, and is now visited once every three weeks or when a break-down occurs.

An interesting fact about the Kish is that the fishing is so good and an abundance can be caught at all times – I say interesting, because when the old light-ship was out there, it was considered to be one of the worst fishing spots on the coast. Curious indeed!

✴ *Fl (2) W 20s* ✴

Kish

Muglins

The danger to shipping posed by the small, granite island known as the Muglins – located around half a mile from the shore in the deep waters of Dublin Bay – was repeatedly and graphically illustrated by the loss of vessels approaching what was once the busy and significant port of Dalkey. The Muglins is around 100 metres long and a mere 17 metres wide, and though uninhabited, it once played host to a couple of exe-cuted pirates. According to a Mr D.A. Chart in *The Story of Dublin* (London, 1907), these two had joined the crew of a ship, murdered the captain and passengers somewhere out in the Atlantic, and made off in a boat with their booty. Miraculously, they reached Waterford Harbour, at which point their luck ran out, and before long they found themselves dangling from the end of ropes in Dublin's Stephen's Green. Just as high-waymen were left to swing at crossroads, marine criminals were at that time exhibited at the entrances to harbours, and such was the fate accorded to the aforementioned pirates. But following objections from a section of the Dublin citizenry, the remains of these two ruffians were transferred to the Muglins, where they were displayed as a warning to others who might be tempted to go for easy money on the high seas.

In 1873, Captain W. Hutchinson, the harbour master at Kingstown – as Dún Laoghaire was once called – wrote to the Board of Trade to suggest a light for the Muglins. The Board was sufficiently interested to request particulars of lost ships, and Captain Hutchinson provided a list of twelve vessels known to have fallen foul of the Muglins. But rather than construct a light on the Muglins, the Board's inspector, Captain Hawes, recommended the raising of the light at Kingstown East by 40 feet, and a sector of the light to be focussed on the Muglins – a good idea, perhaps, but one not acted upon. Time passed and yet more shipping came to grief on the Muglins. Meetings were held and plans drawn up, but it would be several years before work finally commenced on the construction of a 30-foot-high, stone, conical beacon on the Muglins. It was painted white, and would later have a red centre belt added. The year of its establishment was 1880, a full seven years since Captain Hutchinson's request for a signal to protect shipping.

Another 26 years elapsed before a light was established on the Muglins. The red light was initially powered by oil gas, but underwent several conversions before electrification in 1997, when its range was increased to 11 nautical miles. Then, as now, it flashed every 5 seconds.

Like many a beacon, the Muglins grew up to become a lighthouse. Prior to 1979, the Muglins was categorised as a lighted beacon. But in the same year that His Holiness Pope John Paul made his historic visit to Ireland, history was also made on the Muglins with the conferring of lighthouse status on the beacon. At that point, the light on the Muglins was altered from red to white. ✳*Fl W 5s*

There are three lighthouses on Wicklow Head, but neither of the two towers visible from the road that traverses the terrain from Wicklow town to the Silver Strand now operate. On my first visit there, I had much difficulty in locating the entrance point to this particular lighthouse. To get to the lighthouse proper, take the coast road from Wicklow town and – going very slowly – look out for a partially concealed red gate (all Irish Light gates are red) just before you come to the first of the Silver Strands. This gate is not easy to find and is nearly always closed. I do not know what the position is now regarding driving down there, but it would be wise to abandon the car and take a walk over the magnificent headland which is Wicklow Head. On the way, note the well-preserved octagonal tower which commands the head. This former lighthouse was designed by John Trail, engineer to the Revenue Commissioners, a

Wicklow Head

body which preceded, by many years, the present Commissioners for Irish Lights. Built in 1781, this magnificent tower has walls 2 metres thick and is almost 9 metres wide. Where the brick dome is now to be seen, candles were actually used for lighting purposes – helped, of course, by some form of reflectors. The tower is still in use as a daytime navigational aid. The remains of an old cottage nearby point to the possible existence of another cottage-type light at some earlier period. A similar cottage-type light is also to be found on the Old Head of Kinsale. These early lights were most unusual in that they were actually braziers set into the roof of the cottage, and fuelled by coal or other such flammable substances. These fires, of course, needed constant tending – quite a task.

On 10 October 1836, lightning struck the octagonal tower at Wicklow Head, setting fire to it. All the floors and much of the equipment were gutted, rendering it inoperable as a functioning lighthouse. By this time, however, it had become apparent that the light from the tower tended to be obscured by the heavy mists that hung over the head. Although the tower nearby – with the decapitated top – was much lower in height, this light was also obscured by mists.

For a long time, there were actually two lighthouses operating simultaneously on Wicklow Head, so as to distinguish it from the lighthouse on the Baily. Today, Wicklow Head can boast that four lighthouses have been sited there. The present lighthouse was built in 1818 and, though a more modest building than its predecessors, its position is far more effective given its uninterrupted view seaward, and because it is clear of any promontory and at a much lower level. Apart from the light, the station also had a modern lookout system whereby the unmanned Codling lightship, the nearby Lanby buoy and other smaller buoys could be monitored. The range of the present light is 23 nautical miles, and it has a character of three white flashes every 15 seconds. The height of the tower is 14 metres, and the light is 37 metres above high water. Light sources on the head ranged from candles through incandescent to the present-day electric light, which came into operation on 31 March 1976.

Numerous lighthouse families have spent many years at Wicklow Head. I have always considered it a lonely station, and it is hard to conceive of the thriving town just over a mile away. In 1974, the lighthouse became relieving. From then until 31 May 1994, six keepers, in rotation, manned the lighthouse and the watch tower. But on that last day of May 1994, the dreaded automation struck, and all that remains of a once-thriving community is a lone attendant who actually lives in Wicklow town. Brendan Conway, a lightkeeper with 35 years' experience, is nevertheless happy to be the sole guardian of this lonely outpost, and the fact that he is originally from Wicklow makes his job all the more attractive.

All is not lost regarding the decimation of the head. Plans of the Irish Landmark Trust are well advanced for revamping the octagonal tower. It is intended to renovate the building and to lease it to anyone who wants to get away from it all, and who will appreciate the privilege of saying they spent their holiday in a disused lighthouse. ✳*Fl (3) W 15s*

Tuskar

So, finally, we arrive at the last lighthouse on our itinerary around the coast. It is hardly likely that any of my companions for this itinerary are going to find themselves stranded on the Tuskar Rock except, of course, in the line of duty.

Tuskar – a stark, granite, white-painted tower atop a low-lying flat rock – was built in 1815. During its erection, many of the workmen were drowned when a freak wave washed away a hut housing 24 men.

Tuskar

Ten survivors clung onto the rocks for two days awaiting rescue. These men not only finished Tuskar, they went on to build other lighthouses, including Inishtrahull in Donegal – hardy and durable men, indeed. I wonder do the hordes of travellers who use the port of Rosslare ever spare a thought for the efforts that went into the erection of a lighthouse on such a forbidding and treacherous coastline. A low-lying rock like the Tuskar must have posed tremendous tidal problems, and the short time – just four years – it took to build it must have been something of a record.

In the old days – before the advent of reliefs by helicopter – the Tuskar seemed to be forever in the news, mainly due to long overdues. Graphic accounts of stranded and starving lightkeepers were common in the media, and so much the better if the overdue happened around the Christmas period. Yet many other rock stations – such as Slyne Head, Eagle Island and Blackrock in County Mayo – had more numerous and far longer overdues than the Tuskar ever had, though none of these were deemed newsworthy as this famous lighthouse. It was suspected that the eager diligence of a local reporter played a major part in this exposure. Incidentally, I have yet to hear of a lightkeeper dying of hunger. I have spent periods of up to ten weeks on various rock stations and I never went hungry. All rock stations carried enough emergency rations for a long time and, apart from the inevitable lack of variety, many of us fared a lot better than we ever did at home.

✸ *Q (2) W 7.5s* ✸

Epilogue

Lightkeepers were a rare breed, and now, unfortunately, with the advance of ultra-modern nautical technology, their presence as guardians on those lonely outposts which have served the mariner faithfully for hundreds of years is no longer required. Automation has taken over and, I might add, with almost indecent haste.

With the human element gone, does the mariner now feel more isolated out there on the brinny, knowing that all the technological data in the world cannot possibly replace one keen eye with a telescope?

With their passing, the coast has become that much the poorer. To us transient technicians en route to spend a few weeks in places like the Old Head of Kinsale, Loop Head and Mizen Head, it was almost like home from home. A simple phone call meant the fire was on, the kettle boiling, light's warmth, humanity.

A unique way of life has been lost forever, and now the rabbits on Inishtrahull, the puffins on the Skelligs and the terns on Rockabill have it all to themselves. Surely, won't even they sometimes wonder whatever happened to those strange creatures from another world who inhabited their domain for so long; creatures who suddenly packed their belongings, closed the lighthouse door and vanished without trace, forever.